THE FOUR LEGS OF THE TABLE

Raymond Ackerman's simple,
straight-forward formula
for success

as told to
Denise Prichard

Denise Prichard, sadly, passed away on 15 March 2005,
two days before this book was launched.
I remember her with warmth and admiration and
deepest gratitude.

Raymond Ackerman

First published in 2005 in southern Africa by
David Philip, an imprint of New Africa Books (Pty) Ltd,
99 Garfield Road, Claremont 7700, South Africa
www.newafricabooks.co.za

Second Impression 2005
Third Impression 2005
Fourth Impression 2005

ISBN 0 86486 617 8

Editing: Sean Fraser
Proofreading: Tessa Kennedy
Layout and design: Charlene Bate
Cover design: Peter Bosman

Printed and bound in the Republic of South Africa by
Shumani Printers

This book is for Wendy – my constant friend, tireless champion and fiercest critic.

With deep love and sincere thanks.

Excerpts from some of the hundreds of letters received in response to *Hearing Grasshoppers Jump*

Since I started Hearing Grasshoppers Jump *I have not been able to put it down. It is so exciting and reads like a thriller. R Topol*

I have never been quite so inspired ... I read Hearing Grasshoppers Jump *five times. O Suleman*

I have just finished reading Hearing Grasshoppers Jump *and feel that many SA politicians and businessmen could take a leaf out of Raymond Ackerman's book. C Keep*

As a senior lecturer in History, I have read many books in my life, but Hearing Grasshoppers Jump *surely ranks among the best.*
Dr H Terblanche

I felt I had to take the time to write to you and tell you how much I enjoyed reading Hearing Grasshoppers Jump. *It was most inspiring and I am sure I will be quoting from the book for a long time to come.*
A Winde, Western Cape Provisional Parliament

Thanks for the great changes this book has made to my personal and business life. G Pretorius

I work in a family business and would like to tell you how Hearing Grasshoppers Jump *inspired and motivated me. C Rocuzzi*

I broke the story of the "secret" Olympic contract in one of my "City Diary" columns, and found the chapters on the Olympic bid in Hearing Grasshoppers Jump *made riveting reading.*
T Robinson

Having read Hearing Grasshoppers Jump – *which is full of insights, events and tragedies – again shows that corporate social responsibility is an integral part of Pick 'n Pay policy.*
R. Waarderburg

I was particularly fascinated how you correlated your experiences with the unfolding of the historical events in our country. B Coetzee

Contents

Acknowledgements

The Four Legs of the Table has presented all who have been involved in its publication with special challenges. Like its predecessor, *Hearing Grasshoppers Jump*, it has taken two years of solid work to produce.

Denise and I adopted – and discarded – a number of formats before we opted for what might seem the obvious one. We sent each other up the proverbial wall many times, but we worked together as a team. I certainly appreciate her ability, patience and dedication in writing this second book for me.

Now that the final result has been published, I also wish to thank Brian Wafawarowa's team at New Africa Books (of which David Philip is an imprint), for their enthusiasm.

Special thanks also go to my daughter Suzanne and to my wife Wendy for their initial reading of the manuscript and for their early constructive comments.

No list of thanks prefacing a chronicle based around the building and consolidation of Pick 'n Pay could ever be complete without acknowledging the dedication, vision and leadership of the company's present CEO, Sean Summers. Or without acknowledging *all* the other Pick 'n Pay people – both past and present – who have played such a vital role in the success of the business.

I would also like to acknowledge and thank my five mentors, chronicled in the first part of this book. Without them and many other wonderful advisors over the years, the 'Four Legs of the Table' would never have stood secure.

Foreword

About a year after the launch of my biography *Hearing Grasshoppers Jump*, whose success had surprised and delighted us all, my publisher's marketing team dropped an idea like a pebble into a pool that had hitherto been calm and unrippled.

'And now,' they said, casually, 'what about another book?'

Another book!

Owing to a particularly taxing run of business and personal complications, it had taken me two years to decide on writing the first book – an account of the life and times of myself, my family, and Pick 'n Pay, the business we had forged with our colleagues. Following the decision to go ahead, Denise Prichard and I had worked for a further two years on producing *Hearing Grasshoppers Jump* for publication.

Once the suggestion of a second book was raised, I instantly began to think about the people – numbering in the hundreds – who had so kindly written to me about my biography, often wanting to know more about the practicalities of building Pick 'n Pay. Since *Hearing Grasshoppers Jump* was plainly *not* a biography of Pick 'n Pay, there were apparently many details about the business that readers, especially students, wished to know.

The pebble tossed into the waters – the germ of the idea of a second book – soon generated ripples. Before long, Denise and I were back to meeting on Wednesday mornings to talk, argue, debate and record material for what has become *The Four Legs of the Table*: a second book born of a meeting called to review the marketing of a first.

This book sets out to share the essence – the 'life and soul' – of both the founding and the building of the company called Pick 'n Pay that I had purchased in 1967 as a new career option. I was, at the time, unemployed and in urgent need of a fresh source of income to support my family – a wife and four small children.

In so doing, I unknowingly began what would emerge as my life's work: building Pick 'n Pay, with my family and colleagues, into the South African retail phenomenon it is today, with a staff numbering over 40 000 people and a turnover (in 2004) of R29 billion.

When I acquired the first four Pick 'n Pay stores in 1967, at the age of 36, I had already travelled quite a long road in retailing. I started out, straight from university, working my way up from the lowest levels in Ackermans, the drapery-cum-department store chain that my father, Gus Ackerman, and three friends had started in South Africa after the First World War.

The aftermath of the First World War provided Ackermans with the consumers and the local conditions the chain needed to get established and gain a nationwide foothold. On the other hand, the difficult trading conditions that emerged in South Africa at the end of the Second World War brought Ackermans to a point where survival hinged on either borrowing large amounts of capital or selling out.

Greatermans – the South African chain that had been so named because its owners' aim was to become 'greater' than Ackermans – succeeded in purchasing Ackermans in 1945 since my father had elected not to borrow heavily to retain ownership. At that time I was at school, still under the close tutorage of my father as an Ackermans trainee. Much later, when new owners Greatermans offered me a job working with them in Johannesburg, my father urged me to join, as he truthfully if painfully put it, the new 'First Team'.

Soon afterwards, Greatermans launched a small, experimental chain of free-standing supermarkets which they named Checkers. After traversing a bumpy road fraught with obstacles in my career with Greatermans, I was eventually appointed General Manager of Checkers. By the time I parted company with Greatermans in 1966, Checkers had mushroomed from four small stores into a thriving nationwide chain of 85 supermarkets.

In the process of playing my part in directing the thrilling business of building Checkers, I came into contact with the brilliant theories and practices of marketing giants Bernardo Trujillo of the USA and Swiss socialist retail magnate Gottlieb Duttweiler. These two triggered what was to become the quest of my life during the 1950s and early 1960s as I sought the means by which the business brilliance of Trujillo and Duttweiler might be combined with the earlier lessons in commerce I had learned from my father and, in my undergraduate years, from Professor WH Hutt. To these I added the life-guiding principles of Dr Viktor Frankl, a luminary post-Second World War thinker, whose work had affected me tremendously.

When I was introduced to the model that could support both the business and the life-guiding philosophies I so admired and, at the same time, provide the *practical* means by which to run an efficient, profitable business based on the pursuit of consumer sovereignty – the model of the Four Legs of the Table – my quest was almost fulfilled. All I lacked at that stage was an arena in which I would have free reign to put it all to the test.

In theory, the model was thrilling, dynamic, packed with possibility and promise: but would it, could it, work in practice?

When fortune placed Pick 'n Pay in my path and the money to buy it was scraped together in a cobbled plan, I was able to leave behind the thwarted years spent trying to implement methods I had learned from my mentors. Try as I might, the people who controlled my working life up to that time had remained solidly convinced that running a business according to the model of the Four Legs of the Table was a notion deficient in both merit and logic; nothing more than a fanciful product of my over-zealous youth.

But, in 1967, Pick 'n Pay became ours, our family's fresh start, our resurgence in a small way from the long-disguised but keenly felt disappointment of losing Ackermans. Released from the vagaries of my career with Greatermans, here, at last, was an arena in which it might be possible to *prove* that pouring energy and enterprise into building an ethical business on the Four Leg model, dedicated to the pursuit of consumer sovereignty and driven by imperatives above the mere making of money, could not only work, but work magnificently.

As, indeed, the successful evolution of Pick 'n Pay so proved.

Precisely how I came to be enlightened by the ideas and instructions of the five mentors who shaped and sustained both my personal and my business life, forms the first part of the three-part narrative that follows. The second part concentrates on highlighting the particular points of difference that we have applied to building Pick 'n Pay according to our model of the Four Legs of the Table.

The third and final section outlines my own tried-and-tested formula for finding ways forward – the formula that helped me decide to gamble on opening my own chain of supermarkets when I hesitated at a crossroads in my life.

In compiling this book, I acknowledge humbly and with gratitude the contributions of all the people whose ideas, commitment, judgement, work and loyalty have woven the fabric from which the company has been fashioned.

I might be the chairman of Pick 'n Pay, but *all* the people of Pick 'n Pay who once worked or who continue to work with us today – employees, managers, directors, trusted advisors, family and friends – are the company's past, its present and, most certainly, its proud future forward.

Cape Town
January 2005

Forged in Fire
My five mentors

The account that follows retraces the steps I took on
the journey towards melding the philosophies and ideas
of my five life mentors

- Professor WH Hutt
- Gustave Ackerman
- Bernardo Trujillo
- Gottlieb Duttweiler
- Dr Viktor Frankl

into the model on which Pick 'n Pay has been built and
is sustained.

These are the sources of inspiration, the bedrock on
which both my personal life and my career have rested.
I gleaned the knowledge to build my business from the
teachings and experiences of these mentors, but took
in, too, in liberal measure, much else of enduring worth
that has proved infinitely more valuable than mere
business prowess.

"A Customer is the most
important visitor on
our premises.
He is not dependent on us.
We are dependent on him.
He is not an interruption
on our work.
He is the purpose of it.
He is not an outsider on
our business.
He is a part of it.
We are not doing him a
favour by serving him.
He is doing us a favour by
giving us an opportunity
to do so"

MAHATMA GANDHI

Consumer sovereignity is central to the model of the 'Four Legs of the Table' on which the success of Pick 'n Pay is based – a model developed from the teachings and example of five mentors.

1

A visionary economist, Professor WH Hutt

PROFESSOR WH HUTT was an unlikely looking revolutionary but, within the confines of South African economic teaching during the late 1940s and early '50s, that is precisely what he was. A mild-looking man with the power to galvanise student audiences, he had come to teaching via an unconventional route. The rough world of real business had chewed on Professor Hutt and spat him out; he came to teaching having failed as a businessman.

> Inevitably, therefore, when Professor Hutt introduced the concept of consumer sovereignty and explained its place in commerce, I was instantly captivated.

But, like the best of all teachers, experience was grist to his mill. Unlike those academics whose formulas and case studies originate on the pages of books, Professor Hutt knew that of which he spoke.

And what he spoke of most, were iniquities.

He railed against the then new political dispensation – soon to be labelled apartheid – not only because of moral objections to any system based on racial superiority, but also because he believed that holding South Africa's difficult, post-war, emerging economy to ransom by limiting its every aspect according to the philosophy of racial separation was a long-term recipe for disaster. The system of apartheid, according to Professor Hutt, worked directly against the release of economic energies because its policies decreed that white people should be productive and non-white people not.

When I registered for first-year studies at the University of Cape Town in 1949, I was drawn towards medicine far more than to economics, the degree course for which I actually enrolled. This perverse choice would have been easy to understand if I was to lay later claim to a commercial inheritance but, by the time I entered university, the chain of stores my father had built – Ackermans – was already sold, an insignificant loss when seen as part of the fallout from the Second World War, but a hugely significant loss to our family.

So it was that when I enrolled to study commerce at university, although I did not *think* that I felt particularly drawn to the world of business, my past decreed otherwise. The instincts of trade had been etched onto my genetic blueprint over generations, but idealism over-ruled realism at the start of my university career and I badly needed to find some reason, above a genetic predisposition, to

---

Professor WH Hutt (1900–1988)

As Professor of Commerce at the University of Cape Town between 1931 and 1965, Professor WH Hutt was a fierce opponent of monopolistic practices, a champion of the rights of ordinary people and a pioneer thinker on the role of trade unions in South Africa. He was among a minority who correctly speculated from the beginning of the National Party's 46-year governance of South Africa (1948–1994) that economic rather than purely political forces would ultimately defeat apartheid.

Heralded as 'Economist of the Century' by the *Wall Street Journal*, it is surmised that only Professor Hutt's relative obscurity while he lived and worked in a South Africa that was then isolated from the rest of the world enabled the Keynesian theories – on which the West's economic policies were based for four decades – to gain ascendancy as economic gospel over those of Professor Hutt.

An authoritative author in his field, Professor Hutt was Professor Emeritus at the University of Dallas, Texas, USA, where he resided until his death in 1988, aged 88.

---

explain why I, at 18 years of age, was pursuing a course in commerce against all my better instincts.

I could not truthfully claim that anyone – and most particularly not my father – had exerted any influence at all on my choice of degree. Indeed, in those days when career guidance and counselling were subjects yet to be invented, and given my father's firm belief that the end result was all and how you got there was up to you, I had been left to make my academic choices entirely alone.

But, although I was not compelled to do so, I did feel bound by a sense of loyalty to follow a path at university that would acknowledge how much I respected my father's business endeavours. I wanted that austere, remote, Victorian-principled man, who silently suffered in the belief that he had sacrificed his children's birthright with the sale of Ackermans, to understand that I admired all that he had done right in business above the few things he had done wrong.

Outside of lectures, I took to meeting Professor Hutt for long, involved conversations. I was attracted to his unfashionable theories because, although they were unconventional in nature, they were also clearly pragmatic. Later hailed by the *Wall Street Journal* as 'Economist of the Century', Professor Hutt was at best ignored by his colleagues during his tenure at the University of Cape Town, and, at worst, vilified as an egghead and a failed businessman.

I, however, remained enthralled by Professor Hutt and his teachings. He talked for hours about the inequalities the system of apartheid had spawned, speculating – prophetically, as it turned out – that economic forces rather than those of pure politics would one day see apartheid out of the door.

In the vanguard of liberal thought, Professor Hutt's opinions on labour unions and their role in modern economies were decades in advance of their time. He believed that repression of unions was counterproductive because, properly harnessed, the power of organised labour could be used positively – better within than without management structures, he wisely thought. In post Second World War, early 1950s, Calvinistic, conservative South Africa, such thinking was revolutionary, extremely so; unions were perceived by authority as threats, dangerous beasts that needed secure caging if they were not to break their restraints and go on the rampage.

At that stage in my life, while I listened, listened and listened to Professor Hutt, I questioned whether commerce and industry needed unions. According to my reasoning then, if the government of the day was running an efficient economy and if employers were acting fairly and rewarding employees reasonably, what purpose did unionism serve?

In the course of my commercial career I have come to different conclusions about unionisation within the South African economy, despite having had some bruising and mutually destructive confrontations with labour unions in the 1980s and '90s. Today I realise that in the many-layered, complex society that we have in South Africa, the role of the labour unions, in a historic and a contemporary context, is driven by so much more than pure labour issues, as indeed is commerce and industry itself.

The concept of consumer sovereignty

Throughout my undergraduate years, I remember being constantly surprised and stimulated by the daring of Professor Hutt's theories. His lectures and conversations launched my lifelong interest in the wider influence of economics. Above all else, however, it was for the esoteric truths he taught me – truths that at last gave real reason to my present, at that time, and real hope and direction for the future – that I am most grateful.

Although I had settled into undergraduate life with equanimity and enthusiasm, finding the liberal, cosmopolitan University of Cape Town campus refreshing and stimulating after the struggles of my last years at school, the thought that I could find no real *reason* for following the course I was on, above equipping myself to run a business someday, still nagged at the back of my mind. Inevitably, therefore, when Professor Hutt introduced the concept of consumer sovereignty and explained its place in commerce, I was instantly captivated.

According to Professor Hutt, authorities worldwide sustained concerns about the lives and interests of ordinary people only for as long as it took to secure their votes. Once elected, governments and the big corporations with whom they were inextricably linked had bigger fish to fry than issues of interest to consumers.

In a vicious circle of entrenched interest, monopolies and cartels worked to bolster big businesses, whose taxes and donations funded the legislators who allowed monopolies and cartels to thrive. Consumers stood outside the magic circle since, beyond polling days, their interests were of no consequence to anyone – unless commerce itself took consumer rights as its real moral imperative, and stood up and spoke out on their behalf.

The case for moral obligation as a business principle was novel at that time. As one of the band of converted students who took Professor Hutt's concept of consumer sovereignty to heart, I knew that I had heard the foundation upon which I would be able to build a sound reason for choosing a career in business. There was no automatic division between caring and making profits, Professor Hutt explained, because if profit-making became the goal to the exclusion of caring, chances were good that no profits would be made anyway. Profits flowed from having a goal and a moral mission.

All this was fine and clearly good, but even as I began to discover a compelling reason for pursuing a career in commerce, I retained some serious misgivings about the practicalities. The plain trouble with championing the rights of consumers and building a business based on caring was that, fine as those ideals unquestionably were, they seemed more than a little fragile when ranged against what I knew – bitterly and at first-hand – to be the ruthless cut and thrust of retail trading.

Traversing the gentle paths of running a caring business would be a risky venture in the rough, tough world of real trading, where competitive opponents, who did not waste time nurturing such fine ideals, always waited in ambush.

By the time I graduated, I knew that I not only had an instinct for trading, but fierce ambition too. As I went out into the world with my degree tucked under my arm, three years of Professor Hutt's tutorage had convinced me beyond question that there *were* reasons for pursuing a career in commerce that went beyond mere financial gain.

But the nagging question of *why* had now been replaced by the equally perplexing one of *how* – how to bridge the divide between theory and practice. I was still far from discovering, in the USA and in Switzerland, proof that moral stands and profitable business could make perfect partners that cohabited happily in enterprises auditors clapped hands over.

For the time being, however, when I fretted and worried over the question of how philosophy could be intertwined with practicality to create a sound framework for running a successful business, all I seemed to have were pieces of an alluring but complicated puzzle.

Lessons from life mentor Professor WH Hutt

- The concept of consumer sovereignty.
- The obligation of trade and industry to fight for the rights of consumers.
- The powerlessness of consumers against big business and governments.

2

Learning from my father, Gustave Ackerman

'I TRUST,' said my father severely, in a tone that meant he didn't, 'that you went around and shook hands with everyone at your store and told them you were going on leave?'

I had not, as my awkward silence and glum face clearly indicated. So it was that the next morning found me, bright and early, at my father's insistence, back in the Ackermans store where I was working a painfully slow passage through every aspect of the business, learning from the bottom up. I returned as cheerlessly as I had cheerfully left the night before and, reminded of my manners, waited until everyone had arrived at work, then went around shaking hands, as I should have done the night before.

My father had by this time sold Ackermans, but remained on as a director of the vibrant drapery-cum-department store chain he had founded in partnership with two friends, Sam Kirsch and Leon Segal, and in financial partnership with Morris Mauerberger. Retailing, one might say, was in his blood. My grandfather, Meyer Ackerman, had arrived in South Africa during the nineteenth

> It is for his pioneering belief in the virtue of courtesy, as an employer and as a trader, that my father occupies a place of special respect among my life mentors; the standards of courtesy I know and practise, I learned from him.

century, along with thousands of similarly placed penniless and largely uneducated compatriots. Being energetic and enterprising as well as desperately poor, he soon built a successful ostrich-feather export business, on the proceeds of which his wife and two sons – my father and his younger brother Mitchell – eked out a meagre living.

In 1902, Meyer Ackerman died suddenly, leaving his wife and two sons nearly destitute. Bent on survival, they set off for Cape Town, then a plague-infested city struggling to cope in the aftermath of the South African (Anglo-Boer) War. The city had developed a siege mentality as a result of the war and resented the droves of new arrivals who came to try to make a living there.

In a climate of barely concealed hostility, my grandmother opened a small shop selling fruit, sweets and vegetables, in which both her sons were expected to help after school. As the eldest surviving son, my father felt responsible for his mother and younger brother, and soon abandoned school altogether in order to earn more. In these inauspicious circumstances, my father not only survived but went on to found a very successful business.

Gustave Ackerman (1894–1966)

My father, Gustave (Gus) Ackerman, was born in South Africa, the elder son of Lithuanian émigré Meyer Ackerman and his wife, Esther. Gus Ackerman, along with two friends – Leon Segal and Sam Kirsch – founded a drapery-cum-department store chain called Ackermans in Cape Town at the end of the First World War.

As Ackermans expanded, the 1s/11d price tag synonymous with the chain became a byword in South Africa, and even unrelated items that cost 1s/11d became known as 'Ackermans'. By the time Ackermans was sold in 1946, it had grown into a nationwide chain, and many of Gus Ackerman's innovative marketing devices – designed to capture consumer interest and maintain trading vibrancy, such as treating both his staff and his customers with unfailing courtesy – have since become common currency in modern retailing.

Gus Ackerman died in Cape Town in 1966, aged 72.

Belying the austerity of his stern Victorian exterior, my father traded with great verve and energy. He instinctively understood the importance of excitement and pace in retailing and introduced South African consumers to marketing tactics and promotional plans that had them clamouring to sweep up armfuls of Ackermans' famed 1s/11d bargain buys. Many marketing devices, still familiar today, made their debuts in early Ackermans stores. When my father first tried them, they epitomised the spirit of bold commercial venture.

When the Greatermans Group bought out Ackermans in 1945, my father's enterprise had become a household name, known nationwide. The combined effects, however, of difficult war-time trading conditions and the long-term results of an early, injudicious financial arrangement made it impossible for him to hold onto the chain he had built with tenacity, hard work and flair.

The name 'Ackermans' was retained by the Greatermans Group for the goodwill it engendered among consumers, who continued to flock in after the buy-out. Ackermans' customers had grown to love the carnival atmosphere of the endless sales and promotional events that defined the marketing strategies of the Ackermans chain in my father's hands. Just as their parents had fallen for the flagship Ackermans 1s/11d price tag in the 1920s, so the next generation responded warmly and continued to support Ackermans after Greatermans bought it out in the '40s.

Courtesy and a proper respect for cash

It is for his pioneering belief in the virtue of courtesy, as an employer and as a trader, that my father occupies a place of special respect among my life mentors; the standards of courtesy I know and practise, I learned from him. South African retail history acknowledges my father's vigour and vision as a retailer, but his concepts of courtesy were not given the credit they merited, mainly because, in common with each of the mentors who have shaped my life, his ideas were in advance of his times.

When I went to work for Ackermans in the early 1950s, I had already witnessed striking Ackermans employees spitting at my father as he walked to his office during the Second World War because he was a Jewish employer. I remembered how saddened he was by that unseemly behaviour, but how it did not sway him from his commitment to treat his staff courteously.

One day, I would draw deeply on the memory of my father's dignity when Pick 'n Pay and our treasured customers faced similar provocation from mobs of strikers. I count the coaching in matters of courtesy that my father taught me as among the most valuable and enduring of my entire career – although, I have to say, there were times when endurance, in this context, assumed a more trying aspect.

The same deep-seated family loyalty that had nudged me into majoring in commerce at university persuaded me, as a graduate, to take a job as a trainee manager in the Ackermans Group, where my father retained a managing directorship. I can recall my first day there as clearly as if it were yesterday: I arrived bright and early, in a pressed suit and starched-collar shirt, bursting with energy and the importance of my creditable new degree, expecting to receive instructions of note. After my first day at Ackermans, recollections of how I had imagined my first day at work compared to the reality thereof always had the power to summon a wry grimace to my face. I had imagined starting as an understudy in management, but my father had intentions of a humbler nature in mind.

I was instructed, spelled out in my father's brisk, dispassionate voice – in a particular tone that brooked no opposition – to make my way to Ackermans' flagship store in downtown Cape Town, where I was to introduce myself to the manager before taking on the tasks of what would today be termed a 'courtesy officer'. My job was to walk around the shop floor, answer queries, direct customer attention to special items and offer chairs to lady shoppers who looked tired.

Sent smartly off – with admonishing words to the effect that if I did not learn courtesy, I would never learn anything, ringing in my ears – I started the first day of an over-long apprenticeship, as part of which I was required to do little else other than offer chairs to ladies. I never did understand the mysterious process that apparently enabled my father to decide that I had reached a sufficient stage of proficiency in the art of chair-offering, or underwear sorting and labelling, or any of the minor tasks to which I was assigned from time to time, to warrant a minuscule move onwards or, more rarely, upwards.

Although I was not the only trainee yoked to this laboured process of 'learning from the bottom up', it was a plain fact that I spent longer in the menial roles than those less favourably connected. In his strenuous efforts to avoid accusations of nepotism, my upright and unapproachable father erred on the side of extreme caution where his son's career was concerned.

When I did reach the elevated rank of minor management, eventually being put in charge of a small store, I realised that the frustrating journey that had got me there did indeed have merit. I understood the mechanics of running both the front and back doors of a retail business because I had manned both.

Most importantly, through absorbing the attitudes of my father towards issues relating to cash management and the hazards of debt, I had developed a deep and abiding distrust for debt and a healthy respect for the role of cash reserves in the conduct of a healthy business. It was true that my father's aversion to debt sometimes clouded what should have been his better business judgement, but as I worked my way painfully upwards in my father's business, I took the merits of being as debt-free as possible and of having healthy cash reserves to heart – where they would stay for the rest of my business life.

I also gained real insight into the problems and frustrations experienced at the lowly end of the employment scale. I, too, had been a low-income shelf-packer and warehouse clerk. However, just as my father had planned, the mind-numbing training process had brought me to a real understanding of the rightful role of courtesy in conducting a business, and the fact that an argument with a customer can never be won – again, creeds from which I have never since departed.

Lessons from life mentor Gustave Ackerman

- The place of courtesy – an unalterable business basic, as applicable to customers as to staff.
- The importance of flair and excitement – the maintenance of a carnival atmosphere – in the conduct of retailing.
- A distrust of debt – in good times, banks fall over themselves to provide finance; in bad times, they are quickest to call in debt. In 1946, it was partly being tied to an injudicious debt obligation that caused my father to lose Ackermans.
- Cash is king. In financial terms, nothing is as vital as having good cash reserves. Cash is power and the ability to make choices and the vehicle through which a retail business can best look after the interests of consumers.

Caught up in the day-to-day bustle of my early career at Ackermans in Cape Town, I had not forgotten the conundrum I came out of university needing to solve. Watching my father covertly, it seemed to me that he embodied some of Professor Hutt's theories precisely. What, after all, was my father if not a caring employer when he went out of his way to treat his staff courteously? What were the sales and promotions that set his tills ringing merrily as the money rolled in if not working examples of consumer sovereignty – great goods at great prices presented in a carnival atmosphere?

When I ventured to suggest that this might be the case, my father of course dismissed any such suggestion as subversive nonsense. Just as when I had tried to debate the theories I brought back from university, he dismissed my enthusiasm as the folly of youth, encouraged by academics without experience of the real world.

'What's the *point* of all this theory, Raymond?' my father would grumble, and I, in turn, soon learned the pointlessness of trying to change his mind.

None of this bantering between us, which went on for years, was any help in my quest to find a common denominator between theory and practice, but when I moved to the Greatermans chain, I at least edged a little closer to the solution I sought.

3

From the master of retailing, Bernardo Trujillo

THE CHEERY MAN perched on the corner of my desk, swinging a jaunty leg back and forth, looked too ordinary to be the herald of my whole future, but that is what he was.

> Half a century after I first saw one of Bernardo Trujillo's presentations, I can still recall the impact of his dynamism.

I was having a desk-bound day at the Johannesburg headquarters of Greatermans in the late 1950s, vainly trying to sort my way through the mountains of papers that were accumulating around the part of the business that concerned me – the Checkers chain of supermarkets. Given the tedious nature of my occupation that day, any diversion would have been welcome, but that fact alone was not sufficient to explain the avid interest with which I greeted my visitor's news. He told me about a series of seminars called Modern Merchandising Methods (MMM), which his company – National Cash Registers – were sponsoring at their centres in Dayton, Ohio, and McAllen, Texas.

As soon as I heard that casual pronouncement, I longed to go. I believed implicitly that there was a future in the mass retailing of food in South Africa, and I knew that my tutor, Professor Hutt, had been absolutely right in his assertion that the pursuit of consumer sovereignty was not the choice of business but its duty.

BERNARDO TRUJILLO (1919–1971)

Bernardo Trujillo was born in Bogota, Colombia, and his influence on modern marketing was of such import that he became known as 'the Pope of modern marketing'. During the 1950s and '60s, Trujillo created inspirational marketing seminars for National Cash Registers in Dayton, Ohio, and McAllen, Texas, which attracted marketers from all over the world.

Flamboyant, feisty and passionate in his marketing convictions, Bernardo Trujillo's teachings enthused the leaders of some of the most legendary retail chains, among them Auchan and Carrefour – the pioneers of modern retailing in France; British benchmark chains Marks & Spencer and Sainsburys; and Australia's Coles and South Africa's Pick 'n Pay.

Even after his death in 1971, at the age of 52, Trujillo retained a prominent place among those marketers of genius whose enthusiasms and ideas made moulds for modern marketing. Through the millions upon millions of consumers whose superior status he identified as the first obligation of retail trade, his influence has proved ongoing and immeasurable.

When I started working for the Greatermans Group in Johannesburg in 1954, South African retailers had yet to catch even an inkling of the impact that the mass distribution of food through the supermarket industry would have on local business. That food had the potential to become the biggest retail business was still largely unrecognised. South African department stores grudgingly gave space to food sections, which generally traded as poor relations, suitably housed in dim basements, subservient to the aristocratic big-margin departments above.

The food sections in department stores were tolerated only because they served as a minor extra convenience for shoppers, who might be inclined to pop down to the basement to purchase a couple of low-margin food items after spending more lavishly on high-margin purchases above.

The major impediment that kept food scrabbling for a foothold on the retail slopes of the 1950s was disagreement over the gross profit margins the commodity ought to command. Those who managed the fortunes of food were fixated by the fact that department-store merchandise mostly realised margins of 35–40 per cent, which was necessary, in view of overheads, to ensure profitable trading. It was impossible to realise a comparable margin on food, so directors sitting sagely around boardroom tables on the upper floors of department stores, quite naturally begrudged giving valuable floor space to a low earner like food.

In department store terms, food lacked logic.

Looking for logic in mass food retailing

When I arrived in Johannesburg at the age of 23 years, the Greatermans Group was cautiously testing the new waters of food retailing. I was assigned to the food department established in their store at Springs, east of Johannesburg, where I worked with Michael Schulman, a young English trainee, both of us under the tutorage of a gifted Greatermans retailer named Martin Fonn.

Despite the lowly status widely accorded to our merchandise, we three young men discovered an unexpected singularity of purpose; each of us believed that misconceptions lay at the heart of the rejection of food as a profitable trading commodity. The trouble was, however, that since we did not know the precise nature of these misconceptions, dealing with them baffled us. So it was that we took to talking together after work, fortified against fatigue by our shared enthusiasm for food. We pored over dog-eared copies of *The Progressive Grocer* – an American publication that exuded excitement from every page, or so it seemed to the turned-on trio burning the midnight oil in Springs, South Africa, in 1954.

When the first real breakthrough in the impasse over gross margins came, it seemed – as is commonly the case when a problem has been turned up and down, shaken and viewed from every angle – to have been nudging us in the ribs, clamouring for attention, all along. If it was necessary to make 30–40 per cent gross margins in order to cover expenses, why not, we co-conspirators wondered, stock food departments with fast-moving items on an 11–12 per cent gross margin, for which expenses could be kept as low as 9 per cent?

Suddenly, as I started to work out in my own mind how the mass retailing of food could come out on the sunny side of profitable retailing, I arrived at the simple truth on which I, in common with major food retailers around the world, have built multibillion turnover chains: in the words of Bernardo Trujillo: *You don't bank percentages – you bank money.*

Sell a thousand tins of beans with a one-cent profit on each tin, and you bank a thousand cents: therefore, although the percentage on the tins of beans might be lower, the contribution to profits is higher. On the evening in 1954 when that particular light went on in my head, a sleeping South African retail giant of the future – one which would trade according to the maxim that low margins could equal high profits – first stirred.

Even as my colleagues and I worried about the contentious bone of gross margins at our store in Springs, the young man who had reluctantly inherited Greatermans from his recently deceased father set off on a trip that would prove as decisive to my career as it would to his. This was Norman Herber, who headed for the USA on a quest to find ways of modernising Greatermans, the chain of capital-intensive stores his father had bequeathed him.

When he returned to South Africa he brought with him a blueprint for the free-standing, cash-transaction supermarkets he had seen trading so vibrantly in the USA. He resolved to graft the American model onto the South African food market – a move that was both bold and courageous, considering the obvious differences between the two locations. Nevertheless, his mind was made up and soon Africa's first free-standing food markets came to trade in Johannesburg as 'Checkers', a name chosen, like the bold yellow-and-black corporate colours adopted for the stores, from their namesake New York cabs.

Believing, quite correctly, that no one in South Africa was qualified to run the chain of free-standing supermarkets Norman Herber envisaged, he hired a British Marks & Spencer man, Bert

Farson, to run the first Checkers supermarkets in South Africa as a pilot project. As my previous experience working in my father's cash-transaction chain of Ackermans stores was considered useful, and as I was still one of the very few people in the company who had any affection for the business of retailing food, I was appointed Farson's aide, the position in which I worked until events again left the role of running Checkers vacant and I was able to persuade a sceptical Greatermans board that I could take over.

Soon after the first Checkers supermarkets opened their doors, I began to worry quietly to myself, for the fact was that those first free-standing supermarkets were causing far less of a ripple on the retail pond than I and my fellow food fanciers had anticipated and hoped for. As sales remained sluggish, I started to wonder whether detractors of the food trade had a point after all.

The trading pattern in those first free-standing South African supermarkets saw customers coming in to look over the new-style stores, at which time they bought a few items. Subsequently, they perhaps returned once more – after which they stayed pointedly, and permanently, away. This less-than-enthusiastic behaviour on the part of consumers naturally proved profoundly unsettling to all our expectations, not least because we did not understand the origins of the painfully apparent local aversion to supermarket-style shopping.

Theoretically, the advantages of supermarkets were many and obvious – for food retailers. Self-service speeded the progress of customers through stores; supermarkets did not offer credit facilities, nor did they take telephone orders or deliver goods, all expensive and labour-intensive operations. Shopkeepers who thought big obviously saw the move towards supermarket shopping as sensible progress; customers did not. What they saw, quite correctly, was a process of elimination, a taking away of services and conveniences such as deliveries and accounts, which they had always taken for granted, in place of which absolutely nothing was offered as compensation.

The obvious antidote to consumers' early aversion to super-market shopping was obvious, or at least it soon became so to me:

we had to offer them the lowest possible prices, both as an obligation in terms of promoting consumer sovereignty and as compensation for sacrificed services.

The key that would open the floodgates to profitable mass food marketing in South Africa was pricing, but the policy-makers who mattered remained cocooned in their department-store mentalities, fixated on attaching inappropriate margins to food. The key, consequently, remained in their collective pockets. Furthermore, these old-style administrators cared more for conventions than they did for consumers.

Since its pioneering days at the end of the nineteenth century, the supermarket industry in the USA had concentrated on improving systems of distribution, on cutting overheads to the bone in order to mass market to the public at the lowest possible prices. In South Africa in the '50s and early '60s, however, the litmus test applied to price cutting revolved around deciding whether or not reductions would upset suppliers and other food retailers. All such deliberations in those days were skewed towards looking after the interests of everyone – except the consumers.

I, in the meantime, remained acutely aware of the necessity for finding a framework into which the philosophies I admired might be married with the realities of retailing. I retained an instinct, a conviction, that the future of mass food marketing in South Africa was assured if only it could be freed from out-dated restrictions and price controls. I fought daily battles with the Greatermans hierarchy over what I thought the future of Checkers should be, but their reasoning was based on a different trading order to mine and, for the time being, there seemed no middle ground.

Early lessons from Greatermans and Checkers
- A lower percentage realised on mass marketed food items could translate into a higher contribution to profits.
- The key to profitable mass food marketing is pricing.

The slow start made by the infant Checkers chain in South Africa caused me to conclude that somewhere, somehow, we were missing vital points. Modelled, as the concept was, according to successful American blueprints for free-standing supermarkets, we had, for some reason, *not* cracked the code that would ignite mass food retailing in South Africa and launch it into profitable orbit – even though there was clearly no other way forward for the local food industry other than through supermarket trading.

The South African supermarket industry's pedestrian start seemed to me to have at its sluggish heart the dilemma that occupied my thoughts endlessly: how the interests of consumers might be served and profits made. Nothing had happened since I left university to make me believe that Professor Hutt had been mistaken when he asserted that 'authority' and big business cared nothing for the interests of consumers, but outside of the academic arena – with its special rules and lack of immediate pressure – something was needed in the real world to marry consumer sovereignty with profitable trade.

I thought about the course my father's business, Ackermans, had taken. He had treated consumer sovereignty as a living entity within his business, although he would have huffed and frowned over taking on such a label. Nevertheless, the respect accorded to consumers through his policy of treating customers with unfailing courtesy – well before most retailers thought it was opportune or even necessary to do so – showed the high regard he had for people who were good enough to shop with him.

By bringing down prices and making shopping for bargains a carnival, Gus Ackerman showed himself to be a prime, if unconscious, champion of consumer sovereignty. But his fear of debt and borrowing caused him, in the end, to lose his good, innovative business. Something had been missing in the balance of Gus Ackerman's company: timid financial management and an early, injudicious accounting arrangement overwhelmed the ideals of well-practised consumer sovereignty.

Since the days I had eagerly devoured information from the American magazine *The Progressive Grocer,* I had retained the belief that the real leaders, the real innovators, in global mass food marketing lived across the Atlantic in the USA. There, I felt sure, were answers to questions we in South Africa had not even formulated. Thus, when I heard the National Cash Registers man mention the MMM seminars, I received the information as news I had been waiting for.

When I was finally able to accept an invitation to attend an MMM seminar, I set off for Dayton, Ohio, as a man on a mission. I went, specifically, to find out for Greatermans what ailed Checkers and what lay behind the pedestrian performance of supermarkets in South Africa. Most importantly, I set off to find out what we could do to put things right.

Modern Merchandising Methods (MMM) seminars

Half a century after I first saw one of Bernardo Trujillo's presentations, I can still recall the impact of his dynamism. My third life mentor always gave the impression that his mind was racing his voice – he had so much to share, so many ideas, opinions, solutions and challenges to deliver. The first MMM seminar I attended was also one of the first in a series that would become legendary: the list of delegates who passed through the beam of Bernard Trujillo's magnetic band reads like a *Who's Who* of global business.

Information, in the hands of talented teachers, can reverberate with promise. When Bernardo Trujillo told us to remember Modern Merchandising Methods as *desirable goods, openly displayed and readily accessible,* using Marilyn Monroe Miller's initials as a point of reference, he gave focus to a fundamental of retailing, although of course the acronym sounds archaic and unacceptably sexist now.

To me, being told that building a business required '10 per cent capital and 90 per cent guts' and that 'rich people love low prices but poor people need them' edged me closer than I had ever been to understanding my own business personality and the personality of the food industry I believed South Africa needed to have.

When the talk turned to the reasons for being in business, a discussion that caused the introduction of the theory of enlightened self-interest, Trujillo clarified the role of the consumer and the obligations of the retailer. Trading according to the dictates of enlightened self-interest began with a business interpreting what it was that consumers wanted – and then giving it to them. That was the reason for being in business. Taking care of all the interests of consumers, being concerned, being involved and fighting for their rights earned their loyalty, which translated in turn into higher sales.

Bernardo Trujillo taught me to fight for the consumer – *Treat the consumer as queen and she'll make you king* – was a telling Trujillo mantra we all came to know well.

As a committed company man, at that time entirely focused on my career with Checkers, Bernardo's quicksilver teaching excited me because I felt it would help me get to grips with the issues impeding the progress of Checkers in South Africa. I longed to get back and put the new-found theories into place, believing that I now had vital parts of a blueprint out of which a better business could most certainly be forged.

But first, at the conclusion of the seminar, I went with my wife, Wendy, who had accompanied me to the USA, on an extended, shoestring-budget trip around the southern states of America. We hopped on and off Greyhound buses, slept in humble motels and introduced ourselves to supermarket owners in sleepy southern farming towns. We told them we were on a working holiday from South Africa and asked if we could work with them in their stores for the experience. The store owners, unfailingly genial and obliging, would set us to work in some department or other. Even in such small towns, there was no doubt that food retailing was as vibrant and adventurous in the USA as it was lacklustre and still somewhat apologetic in South Africa.

Every evening, after returning from our supermarket labours and that night's fast-food supper venue, my young wife and I would bounce ideas off each other, which I compiled into lengthy reports for the Greatermans board back home, certain they would be read with the same avid interest as I had written them.

As it happened, however, my enthusiastic outpourings on a bright new future for Checkers were not appreciated by anyone in South Africa with the authority to make a difference. Most of what I wrote – a blueprint, actually, for the future of Checkers – ended up in waste-paper baskets.

But, like all new converts, I was stimulated rather than daunted by the prospect of opposition and indifference. After all, who could *fail* to see the sense in applying the best methods of the booming American mass food market to our pedestrian South African supermarket chains? The answer, as it turned out, was more people than I could possibly have imagined …

Fighting to implement modern merchandising methods

The South Africa I returned to in the early 1960s, after my first trip to the MMM conference in the USA, was characteristically about to confound again. The decade of the '60s had opened on a note of profound uncertainty. Civil unrest, particularly the Sharpeville massacre of 1960, led politicians and economists across the world to predict that this was the beginning of the end of white rule in South Africa – not before time either, in the opinion of an increasing number of governments and stridently effective anti-apartheid campaigners.

Following the dreadful events at Sharpeville, South Africa's economy was shaken to its shallow fiscal roots when a sizeable sum in foreign capital immediately fled the country. But the conduct of modern South African commerce, like the nation's economic and political fortunes, has always been marked by a combination of strength and vulnerability, often behaving unexpectedly to confounded prediction.

After Sharpeville, the National Party government of South Africa introduced a series of measures so repressive they almost immediately quelled and contained unrest. Soon, relative calm returned. The absence of major outbreaks of violence after the early

'60s encouraged the return of foreign capital, which flowed back as rapidly as it had left. Overseas investors gained the conviction that South Africa was a good risk – paradoxically because, in the eyes of investors, the rest of the African continent was not.

Instead of collapsing into the widely predicted mire of civil unrest and economic ruin predicted, the 1960s saw South Africa enter into the greatest boom in the nation's history up until that time. Industrial expansion was massive, and a mighty influx of immigrants arrived to service it.

When I returned to this surreal society, I too was confounded – by the news that, in my absence, a new man had been appointed to take over my job managing Checkers. Like a fool, I had spent the past months away labouring under an illusion; I had thought that the enthusiastic research, suggestions and solutions sent back to the Greatermans board in South Africa on a regular basis were being read and accepted for what they undoubtedly were – a blueprint for rescuing Checkers from mediocrity.

Far from being convinced, however, the leaders of Greatermans had been irritated – so much waffle from a young man who had lost his head, gone out of control. What Checkers needed, they thought, was a level-headed fellow, and, accordingly, they had appointed my successor.

I should, of course, have walked out of Greatermans at that stage: being deposed in such a shabby fashion did not augur well for the future, but loyalty to my father's old firm prevailed and I accepted defeat and launched unhappily into an era of working randomly where the whims of my employer decreed. I managed children's, men's and houseware departments, tortured all the while by the bitter irony of having to watch the then four-strong chain of Checkers supermarkets floundering on the edge of failure when I believed I had the answers capable of turning the chain around.

I fretted and fumed over all the wasted knowledge at my fingertips – but I did not do so quietly. I wanted to get back into food too badly to accept my substitute role without demur. Eventually, worn down by my persistent representations, the board of

Greatermans let me take over management of the smallest, least profitable of the four-store Checkers chain – on the astonishing condition that I should not attempt to cut prices on branded goods. This was an onerous condition, but I resolved to show the Greatermans hierarchy that I could turn Checkers around.

I began working with my staff towards a Grand Re-opening Day at the dingy little Checkers store, the least profitable of the struggling quartet. Work started as a spirited cleaning and polishing exercise but soon I was planning a subversive discount strategy.

In order to overcome the prohibition on cutting the price of branded goods, we created our own version of house brands by the simple, but wicked, expedient of removing the wrapping from branded goods. We unwrapped branded candles, for instance, tied them into bundles and stuck on plain price labels. We denuded cans of their labels by vigorous scrubbing and were thus able to offer goods at genuinely discounted prices. At that time, the OK Bazaars was having a first, tentative flutter in the house-brand stakes with the small-scale introduction of their Pot o' Gold products. In general, though, the concept of house brands was one that would come into its own more than a decade later.

For the meantime, the unconventionally assembled Checkers house-brand goods on sale on Grand Re-opening Day at my little store were trail-blazers, portents of a massively important trend of the future. To promote the contrived house brands, flashes went up in the store windows – Grand Re-Opening! Special House-Brand Discounts! American-Style Supermarket Specials!

When the store opened its doors on Grand Re-Opening Day, watched by a sceptical contingent of senior Greatermans managers visiting especially for the event, customers did not enter the store in a flood – indeed they did not even enter in a trickle. A silence hung over our shining shelves and piled-up displays of special-price products. Every time I caught the eye of one of my visitors, I sensed what they were thinking – so much for Raymond Ackerman's bright ideas and what a failure, what a flop – so I tried my best to avoid doing so.

As the minutes ticked interminably by and 9 turned to 10 and then 11 o'clock without the sight of a single customer, I began to despair. I must have got it all wrong, and what a fool I would look as a result. These were the miserable thoughts that were whirring around my brain when, quite suddenly, as though an invisible boom had been lifted, people began to arrive, clamouring to claim their bargains. As the atmosphere in the little store at last turned carnival-like, my visitors began to look thoughtful.

The Cinderella store, always just breaking even, barely worth keeping open at all, finally came to the ball dressed in all her finery – that day, between the hours of 11am and 1pm, record takings went into the tills, and that was only the beginning of an outstanding upturn, sustained from opening day forward.

I was enchanted by the whole exercise but, as it turned out, the buyers and accountants who regulated Checkers' supplies were not. A huge amount of fussing and flapping ensued: what would happen when suppliers got to know that their branded goods had been discounted? Supposing other chains assumed Checkers was starting a price war and took exception?

It was the same old song sung to the same old tune – worry about everyone's interests above those of consumers; relegate consumer sovereignty to the bottom of the heap.

Despite the rumblings of discontent, the strategies that had made my Grand Re-Opening Day an ongoing success – the same ones I had been begging Norman Herber to adopt for the whole Checkers chain – finally made my point. It was conceded, none too gracefully, that perhaps I did, after all, have the makings of a recipe that would rescue the flagging fortunes of Checkers and perhaps, therefore, I should be given free reign to try.

Appointed General Manager of the then four existing Checkers supermarkets, I took off running, and was soon sprinting towards the final tally of 85 Checkers supermarkets that would exist by the time I parted company with Greatermans in 1966.

I worked unbelievably hard, and gained gratifying recognition from press and public for my efforts, coping all the while with huge expansion while trying to weave the principles by which I wanted to live and trade into the fabric of the buoyant retail chain Checkers had become.

Fighting for the consumer

Details in my day-to-day working life as General Manager of the Checkers chain were often irksome. I had a set of principles and theories in which I believed, but policy-makers within Greatermans were still miles away from accepting the sense of such a course.

I brooded about the company's administrative structure, which decreed that the person responsible for overall management of the chain's supermarkets – myself – had no say over the prices at which goods were sold in the stores. Although we were supposed to be on the same side, this particularly erroneous policy pitted me against the buyers who were charged with pricing goods in my stores, when we ought to have operated as a team, focused on negotiating the best possible deals in order to sell at the lowest possible prices.

How could our consumers be treated as the retail royals they were supposed to be when pricing structures answered interests other than theirs? The monopolies and cartels against which Professor Hutt had once so roundly railed still held their superior heads high, dictating prices that retailers dared not challenge, on pain of having their supplies cut off.

To my fervently food-orientated mind, engrossed in the process of building and promoting Checkers in the early 1960s, the attitude of my superiors towards cutting prices, or putting promotions in place, or on issues of social responsibility seemed blind, antiquated and plainly counterproductive.

Sometimes, differences in perspective caused matters to come suddenly to boiling point – as happened once when what I thought of as a small but important gain almost cost me my job.

One of the cartels that maintained a stranglehold on the prices of their products were the suppliers of toiletries. To begin with, lines that could be carried on supermarket shelves were autocratically limited by suppliers who did not wish to antagonise pharmacies or disrupt the cosy price-controlling relationship that existed with them.

Supermarket chains similarly maintained a gentlemen's agreement with toiletry suppliers: those lines they were permitted to stock would be uniformly priced from chain to chain.

After a protracted period spent nibbling away at the inevitable resistance to any proposed price-promotion plan I put forward, I finally succeeded in persuading Greatermans to agree to *cut* the prices of certain toiletry lines on Checkers' shelves. Accordingly, certain lines were chosen for discount and advertisements placed to announce this ground-breaking promotion – small and insignificant by today's retail standards, but hugely important as a pioneering venture in the 1960s.

As the advertising campaign broke, a great buzz of anticipation started circulating, whereupon I was urgently summoned to the Greatermans head office where I was flabbergasted to hear that the entire Checkers toiletries discount promotion was to be called off – because opposition chains had cried foul.

I was furious – absolutely furious. It was completely unethical to disappoint consumers on the flimsy premise that other chains had objected. It did not matter that the suppliers were put out, that the other chains felt aggrieved – we had made a commitment to consumers to cut the prices of toiletries for a given period and we therefore had a moral obligation to do so.

This astonishing turnabout so angered me that I threw caution to the wind, announcing that if the toiletries sale did not proceed according to our advertisements, I would resign for the shame of working for a company that failed to keep its word. With that, I turned on my heel and marched out – headed for my golf club, where I proceeded to vent my frustration on a vigorous round.

Back at work, I awaited the call that would tell me that my resignation had been gratefully accepted – but the call never came. Surprisingly, my protest proved effective, although I am certain it was more the spectre of losing consumer respect than the prospect of losing me that did the trick.

Following that first toiletries price-cut, there were other repercussions. Opposition chains muttered darkly about an unstoppable price war starting, one in which suppliers and all traders would suffer. On the topic of consumers gaining, however, there was a conspicuous silence.

The great debate over the discounted toiletries in the '60s, a debate that set the retail industry abuzz, turned on a simple fact that was not only soon lost, but in most instances never surfaced at all. As I had learned in the USA and tried to put into practice in building Checkers, the first obligation (not choice) of retailers was to promote consumer sovereignty – no interest took priority over theirs.

Lessons from life mentor Bernardo Trujillo

- MMM: 'desirable goods, openly displayed and readily accessible'.
- You don't bank percentages, you bank money.
- Rich people love low prices, poor people need them.
- The role of social responsibility (enlightened self-interest) in business.
- Fight for the consumer, and the consumer will fight for you.

Out of a series of confrontations, the perception grew within Greatermans that I was 'difficult', but I believed I was standing up for what was right for Checkers – I was a fiercely loyal employee through all of this – and for consumer sovereignty.

However, I did opt for unconventional methods from time to time, to get what I knew Checkers needed. Each year, for instance, I would wait, biding my time, until the chain's Chief Buyer took his annual leave. Then, with the cat safely away, I would slash prices to the bone on special promotions. Once, brushing aside the anguish of nervous accounts-office underlings and while the Chief Buyer happily, and obliviously, holidayed, I went out and bought a whole fleet of cold trucks to improve the distribution of fresh produce.

Naturally enough, the reckoning always came. I would be summoned to stand before men who spluttered with rage and banged their desks, sending offending invoices – evidence of my independent efforts – flying. In retrospect, I can see that I was insufferable: forever challenging, always wanting discounts, acting on my own independent judgement.

But, wayward and annoying as my tactics might have been, there was no denying the fact that I was a loyal and dedicated company man who saw my job as my career for life – my business mission. There was also the fact that my misdemeanours made money; healthy profits flowed from my errant deeds, which, at the end of the day, silenced detractors.

Greatermans' management structures in the '60s were organised as an authority pyramid. Getting to speak to someone 'above' meant scaling a slope so high, steep and treacherous, people mostly just gave up and went quietly away.

There had to be a better way of treating people, I thought – one that would translate into a better way to run a business. The policies of decentralisation and flat management structures that became pillars of strength to my later endeavours, fundamentally came into being as reactions against the unwieldy, confused and inaccessible structures I worked within at Greatermans up to 1966.

In spite of the frustrations and difficulties of my working life at Checkers, it was a period of wonderful expansion and growth both for the company and for my career The management of Greatermans had shown courage and foresight when they decided to back expansion in strife-torn South Africa. As a reward, Checkers supermarkets fast became the face of suburban food shopping, a fact in which I took enormous pride.

And yet – even as I relished the growing success of mass food marketing in South Africa – I remained aware that the true potential of the South African food industry was evading local retailers. The principle of consumer sovereignty was the beginning, the middle and the end – but what was needed now, I knew in my heart, was a practical model that would provide a system for running a business both ethically and profitably, according to the principles of consumer sovereignty. Driven by fierce ambition,

ambition that was still harnessed to the Greatermans Group despite ongoing differences between us, I knew that if I found the model I sought I would have the blueprint for an unstoppable commercial success.

What I therefore needed – now – were some tools.

So it was as a confident but frustrated, ever-searching young executive that I set off in 1963, bound again for the USA and another meeting with marketing genius Bernardo Trujillo. It was to be, in every classic sense, a date with destiny.

Eureka: the master lesson

Before the morning in November 1963 when Bernardo Trujillo turned the key that opened the door to my future, I had never experienced the feeling of hearing words so important that they stood in front of my eyes like a great bold banner.

But what I heard that morning answered the core business problem that had puzzled me all my adult life. How could theories and philosophies be practically formed into a model capable of running a business that was both ethical and profitable?

I cannot say with certainty why my first hearing of Trujillo's then latest theory – 'The Four Legs of the Table' – affected me so profoundly, but it did. Suddenly, I *knew* I had my answer.

As the master marketer explained, balancing a business on four legs labelled 'Administration', 'Merchandise', 'Promotions/Social Responsibility' and 'People' covered every business base equally, forming four strong pillars that made the enterprise unassailable.

On top of the table sat the reason for the existence of the business below, in the case of a retail organisation, the sovereign consumer. Crucially, each of the four legs had to be equal in strength so as to achieve a proper balance; if one leg was weaker, the table – the business – would develop a dangerous wobble that could become bad enough to topple the entire enterprise.

Although each of the four legs comprised a number of individual components, each was inextricably linked to the performance and wellbeing of the others. An undetected or unremedied problem in any leg had the potential to tip a table, regardless of whether it supported a mega or a mini enterprise.

As soon as I heard this and thought about it, I was instantly struck by its simple, sane sense. Why had my father lost his Ackermans chain in 1946, if not because his business, so dynamic and right in many innovative ways, had become unbalanced by an overcautious financial policy in the first leg of the business – the fatal wobble that toppled Ackermans over and into the hands of its buyers?

Why were there such areas of vulnerability – later also to prove fatal – in the structures of the Checkers chain if not because market share took precedence over consumer sovereignty? Relationships within the organisation were taut; people whose opinions ought to have counted were not heard, consulted or considered. When I first heard word of Bernardo Trujillo's model of the Four Legs of the Table, the Checkers table had already developed an ominous wobble, although it would stand, increasingly precariously, until it finally toppled into a takeover at the beginning of the 1990s.

It was not immediately clear how I could build all the philosophical ideas and theories I had been gathering on Trujillo's four-legged table – but the fact that I had the formula for doing so was now etched in crystal clarity, and I hugged the newfound theory to myself like a long-lost friend. I started to see precisely how to structure business to maintain balance between all four crucial legs and how dependent each leg was on the whole.

Bernardo Trujillo's master lesson

- Balancing a business on four legs labelled 'Administration', 'Merchandise', 'Promotions/Social Responsibility' and 'People' covers every business base equally, forming four strong pillars that make the enterprise unassailable.

4

Introducing a legendary Swiss retailer, Gottlieb Duttweiler

❝ The house, he said, represented his businesses and the heavy defences on windows and door were there in an attempt – futile, as it happened – to stop money he had given away from getting back in. ❞

AS THOUGH HAVING introduced me to the theory of the Four Legs of the Table was not a great enough contribution to my development, Bernardo Trujillo was also responsible for sending me to Zurich in Switzerland to see the legendary retailer Gottlieb Duttweiler, who was my fourth life mentor and a towering influence in my life.

In the early 1960s, Gottlieb Duttweiler was the most provocative figure in European food distribution, a vociferous thorn in the side of authority, whose laws he vigorously and spectacularly challenged on behalf of Swiss consumers.

The history of Gottlieb Duttweiler is a fascinating one in that, with only a tiny amount of capital in his pocket, he founded Migros, today a multimillion-dollar trading concern, as a protest against the high prices merchants were extracting from Swiss consumers.

Starting with a few trucks converted into mobile stores and loaded with just half-a-dozen food staples, Gottlieb Duttweiler traded vigorously on Swiss streets and byways, undercutting established retailers so drastically that they had no choice but to reduce their prices to meet his competition. From these humble beginnings, the Migros Group was ultimately able to reduce the cost of some basic foods by up to 25 per cent.

But it was not only in the area of food distribution that the feisty Duttweiler fermented change. As a man with a passionate belief in the virtue of sharing, he pioneered a cooperative system whereby Migros, then running according to the most sophisticated and efficient methods of distribution and marketing, was handed back to customers to be run for their own profit.

Throughout his tempestuous and committed career, Gottlieb Duttweiler questioned legislation designed to compromise the rights of ordinary consumers. Swiss authorities, unused to insubordination in their ordered land, were astonished and affronted by this upstart, rising from the law-abiding ranks of Swiss citizenry, who dared to challenge laws that they, the rightful authorities, deemed right and proper. Resale price maintenance, as it was applied in Switzerland and later greater Europe, the grip of monopolies and cartels and

GOTTLIEB DUTTWEILER (1888–1962)

A phenomenal, provocative and controversial figure in the history of European retailing, Swiss-born Gottlieb Duttweiler built his vast-volume operation, Migros, on a philosophy of sharing with his staff, his customers and the community. During his working life, Gottlieb Duttweiler never took a salary greater than those paid to his managers and gave preference to suppliers who held similar principles. He famously maintained – and thereby proved the efficacy of the 'enlightened self-interest' theory in business – that the more money he tried to give away, the more flowed back into his businesses as increased profits.

His courage and tenacity in fighting entrenched systems that adversely affected food prices in Switzerland resulted in an overall reduction of 25 per cent in the price of food, which represented a great victory for Swiss consumers.

A committed philanthropist, who started out selling cut-price food from mobile shops to thwart monopolists, Duttweiler's story is one of the most amazing in the annals of modern mass marketing.

their ability to control markets and prices were among the issues Duttweiler successfully challenged in courts of law.

Later, when I was caught up in the complexities of similar legal issues in South Africa during the 1970s, I found solidarity in conjuring up the image of the august Gottlieb Duttweiler facing down Swiss legal authority on behalf of consumers.

Giving above getting

The evidence that profitable enterprises could garner greater rewards when run according to principles higher than the mere pursuit of profits was graphically demonstrated during the first half-hour interview granted to me by Mr Duttweiler. At that time, as I sat across a small desk in front of the gruff and somewhat intimidating retailer, he quickly put some finishing touches to a rudimentary drawing and presented it to me with a flourish.

What he had drawn was a simple picture of a small house. Thick bars had been pencilled in across the doors and windows, each secured with a heavy padlock. I wondered what this meant.

Gottlieb Duttweiler explained: the house, he said, represented his businesses and the heavy defences on windows and door were there in an attempt – futile, as it happened – to stop money he had given away from getting back in.

A business fighting to keep money out?

The idea seemed preposterous. Yet Mr Duttweiler told me unequivocally that the more he tried to give away profits – to charities, to cooperative profit-sharing schemes – the more the money flowed back as increased sales and even higher profits.

At last, the piece of the puzzle that had eluded me since my undergraduate days – how the ethics of consumer sovereignty and social responsibility might be practised within a business without compromising or limiting the horizons of profit – was revealed: the conundrum was solved.

Trading according to the ethics of consumer sovereignty and social responsibility did not limit the horizons of profit, but rather expanded them – to the benefit of all.

As Gottlieb Duttweiler in Zurich, Switzerland, had demonstrated and Bernardo Trujillo in Dayton, Ohio, had said, 'Doing good was good business.'

Lessons from life mentor Gottlieb Duttweiler

- The more money a business gives away, the more money flows back.
- Greater rewards can be garnered from running a business according to principles above the mere pursuit of profits.
- The obligation to face down authority on behalf of consumers.
- The obligation to oppose cartels and monopolies.

A little over three years after I had been through the life-changing experience of absorbing the information that something so simple as the model of the Four Legs of the Table could revolutionise the life and prospects of a business, I had a great stroke of luck.

I was fired.

At the time – September 1966 – this did not seem fortunate at all but, without that unseemly shove, I think I would have remained bound by loyalty to my career with Greatermans, and would consequently not have needed to go in search of the new career that turned out to be ownership of my own small chain, Pick 'n Pay.

As it was, at the age of 35, the abrupt end of my tenure as General Manager of Checkers had me casting around urgently for a fresh start – not least of all because I was not well off financially and had a wife and four small children to support.

When my brother-in-law told me that a chain called Pick 'n Pay, comprised of four small stores, was on the market in Cape Town, I immediately wanted to look them over and hurried down to Cape Town the very next day to do so, consumed by a feeling that this was another journey of destiny.

Just one visit to the four-store Pick 'n Pay chain that owner Jack Goldin – later doyen of the Clicks empire – wished to sell, left me with one overriding conviction: I had to have them. By the early hours of the following morning, after lengthy and intense negotiation, I had agreed to purchase Pick 'n Pay from Jack Goldin for the considerable sum, for the day, of R620 000.

I offered to settle the purchase price as R600 000 in cash, with the remaining R20 000 changing hands in the form of the Raymond Ackerman shares, which I intended to issue as recompense for a six-month hand-over period during which Jack Goldin would work with me in the business.

Accumulating the necessary funds that allowed my family to acquire Pick 'n Pay blurred into a few days of high-tension travail, but on a fine Friday morning in February 1967, with funds raised from vendors and Standard Bank lending the balance, the purchase price of R600 000 was handed over.

Once again, the Ackerman family owned a chain.

This time our chain was called Pick 'n Pay.

5

Viktor Frankl and the search for meaning

'I AM NOT AS GLOOMY about the prospects as most people are, and I feel quietly confident that we [South Africans] are going to ride the storm.' This extract from my diary, written in 1976, stands as a direct tribute to the lessons I learned from the fifth of my life mentors, Dr Viktor Frankl.

In 1976, South Africa was a nation in turmoil. Dreadful riots, particularly in Soweto, to the south-west of Johannesburg, were tearing the country and its people apart, edging the nation inexorably, it seemed, towards civil war. On our borders and in neighbouring countries, war was being waged. South African participation in these conflicts unleashed an unprecedented outpouring of international criticism against us and led to the imposition of sanctions. Meanwhile, compounding the miseries, South Africa's ever-vulnerable economy languished in a slough of despondency.

It was during this time of raw-nerve tension, when every day seemed to bring worse news than the day before, that I leaned most gratefully on the philosophies of Dr Frankl.

Viktor Frankl, a Holocaust survivor, developed the theory that every individual is motivated by the search for meaning and that the

> It was during this time of raw-nerve tension, when every day seemed to bring worse news than the day before, that I leaned most gratefully on the philosophies of Dr Frankl.

39

> ### DR VIKTOR FRANKL (1905–1997)
>
> Viktor Frankl, my fifth life mentor, was an Austrian psychiatrist and psychotherapist who developed the psychological approach known as 'logotherapy', the basis of which was that the primary motivation of an individual is the search for meaning in life.
>
> In 1942, Frankl and his family were sent to the concentration camps where his mother, father and wife perished. As he observed the brutality and degradation around him, Frankl theorised that those inmates who had some meaning in their lives were more likely to survive. After the war, he published the book *Man's Search for Meaning* (1946), which sold some nine million copies in 26 languages.
>
> On a practical level, Viktor Frankl surmised that those individuals who discovered what it was that they really wanted to do and then did it 'to distraction', had the means – through the intensity of their commitment – to find answers to those deep questions that have always engaged mankind.

primary purpose of psychotherapy should be to help the individual find that meaning.

Dr Frankl and his family had been among the hapless Jews of Vienna who were herded out of that city in 1942 and into Nazi Germany's concentration camps. As Frankl observed the brutality and degradation all around him, he theorised that those inmates who had some meaning in their lives, who had hope, were more likely to survive.

In 1946, following his liberation after the Second World War, his slim volume *Man's Search for Meaning,* a work of monumental impact, was published. Here Frankl recorded the story of the camp inmate who loved birds and who climbed every day, craning his neck at the merest chink of light, longing to catch a glimpse of a bird in flight. He told of a carpenter, a man who enjoyed more than anything the smell of newly planed wood, and who closed his eyes and planed imaginary planks, conjuring the smell he loved. There was a pianist who so longed to play again that he 'practised' daily on a piece of cardboard, hearing melodic notes flying from his fingers as clearly as if he had been playing the finest grand piano to a packed concert hall.

All these people survived, Dr Frankl theorised, because they were sustained by hope – they had a meaning to their lives; but when that hope, or meaning, was lost, so too was life.

Man's Search for Meaning also contains the story of a fellow prisoner Frankl had known who confided that he had had a vision which revealed the date on which the concentration camp and its inmates would be liberated. When the projected date came and it was clear that no liberating armies were going to come, the disillusioned prisoner sickened, and was dead by the following morning. Officially, he had died of a latent disease; actually, as hope of liberation fled, Frankl reported, he had died of a broken heart.

Doing to distraction

When I discovered the theories and philosophies of Viktor Frankl, through Patti Havenga Coetzer, life-long friend and student of Viktor Frankl and founder of the Viktor Frankl Foundation of South Africa, I fell upon them with enormous enthusiasm. Although I had no conception above my sensibilities, thank God, of the sufferings of the men who loved birds and wood and music, the concept of meaning supporting life, and hope having the power to give life meaning, resonated with what I had come to realise I was looking for.

Viktor Frankl's pivotal piece of philosophical advice – 'Find out what it is that you want to do, and do it to distraction' – has a layer of meaning that goes deeper than the advice in similar vein that has been given by leaders and achievers throughout history, where total commitment is emphasised as a prerequisite for success. Viktor Frankl's philosophy sees the pursuit of a passion, an activity pursued to distraction, as a starting point from which will flow answers to those enormous, seamless questions that all questing people ask at some stage in their lives.

As the men who loved birds, wood and playing the piano in the concentration camp once discovered, nurturing a passion becomes its own life force, a way in which hope and, therefore, life can be sustained in the face of adversity and through which the deepest questions may be answered.

The philosophies of Viktor Frankl also taught me to understand and appreciate the possibilities of adversity. During periods of great stress and trial in my life – both personal and business – retaining a sense of hope, a conviction that things would get better, made many tribulations more tolerable.

Thus, during the terrible year 1976, I made sense of the pervasive despair that was all around by suggesting, with my colleagues, that if 100 South African companies would adopt policies of equal opportunity and salary on merit, tension could instantly be dissipated. Through that suggestion we, as a company, indicated that we not only hoped in a nebulous fashion that things would get better, but believed that they would – and made a practical suggestion as to how that might happen.

Then there were the years 1994–5, which remain etched into my consciousness as a time of the most concentrated tumult I, and our company, have ever experienced. In 1994, just as South Africa was celebrating the great triumph of having held the country's first all-race democratic elections peacefully and when the nation as a whole basked in a feeling of renewed hope for the future, chaos and upheaval visited Pick 'n Pay, bringing bitterness to the end of our rainbow.

It was a cruel paradox: just when it seemed that the terrible times all South Africans had lived through, and business people had traded through, could at last be put aside in a united effort to build a new South Africa, a dreadful, destructive strike was declared against Pick 'n Pay.

Not content with peaceful picketing and unwilling to restrict confrontation to talks around a negotiating table, striking workers went on the rampage, smashing up stores and terrifying customers. As I watched nightly television news bulletins at that time, footage showing baying mobs vandalising stores and intimidating anyone hapless enough to cross the strikers' paths, as I began receiving deadly serious death threats over the telephone, I had to trawl more deeply then ever before to retain some vestige of hope that there would be a resolution.

At the darkest time, when I had seriously begun to think that everything we had worked so hard to build was going to come down in flames, calling on Viktor Frankl's philosophy around sustaining hope, even in the direst of circumstances, saved me from despair, particularly as another dream – one for which I had worked tirelessly, had largely financed from my family's funds, and had lived and breathed for years – was also coming down in ruins.

Since 1990, in company with my wife and, later, a dedicated team of professionals, we had committed our time, our energy and our money to bringing the 2004 summer Olympic Games to Cape Town.

Up to that point, no event in South Africa's history had ever been so auspiciously starred: the state of our rainbow nation was perfect for such an endeavour, as the world cheered and applauded our peaceful transition from apartheid to democracy and lauded the world's most admired statesman, South Africa's first black president, Nelson Mandela. And, in the case of Pick 'n Pay's involvement in Cape Town's 2004 Olympic bid, this was the greatest exercise in social responsibility upon which the company had ever embarked.

However, as history knows, Cape Town lost that bid to Athens, news of which – coming at a time when I was personally exhausted from plunging all my energies into promoting Cape Town's bid, while also worrying desperately about the strike that was crippling Pick 'n Pay and mourning a sad spate of deaths in our family – was simply devastating.

At that dark time, finding hidden reserves of energy in order to rekindle the fire of hope to fuel fresh optimism that there was a future for both our company and our country, I have the work of Viktor Frankl to acknowledge and to thank.

Frankl's deep philosophical approach helped me make sense of confusion, warded off despondency and allowed me to retain a huge sense of hopefulness for the future all South Africans share.

As for the cornerstone of Frankl's teaching – finding out what you want to do and doing it to distraction – I had the great good fortune to discover as a young man that what I really wanted to do was to promote the interests of consumer sovereignty.

Which, ever since I made that discovery, is precisely what I have done – to distraction.

Lessons from life mentor Dr Viktor Frankl

- Hope is the supreme power, bringing meaning to life; without hope, life itself loses reason.
- Learning to conquer trials and overcome challenges are the gifts rather than the curses of adversity.
- Find out what it is that you want to do, and do it to distraction.

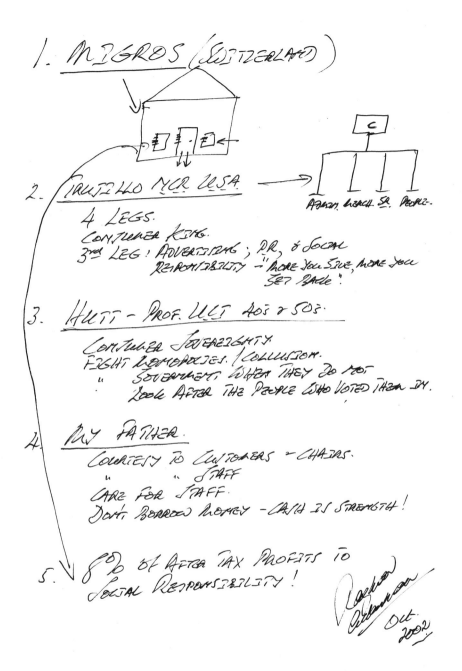

1. MIGROS (SWITZERLAND)

2. TRUJILLO NCR USA →

   ADMIN. BRANCH. SR. PEOPLE.

   4 LEGS.
   CONSUMER KING.
   3rd LEG: ADVERTISING; P.R. & SOCIAL
   RESPONSIBILITY → "MORE YOU SAVE, MORE YOU
   GET BACK".

3. HUTT - PROF. UCT 40s & 50s.

   CONSUMER SOVEREIGNTY.
   FIGHT MONOPOLIES. / COLLUSION.
   " GOVERNMENT, WHEN THEY DO NOT
   " LOOK AFTER THE PEOPLE WHO VOTED THEM IN.

4. MY FATHER.

   COURTESY TO CUSTOMERS → CHAIRS.
   "   "   STAFF
   CARE FOR STAFF.
   DON'T BORROW MONEY - CASH IS STRENGTH!

5. 8% OF AFTER TAX PROFITS TO
   SOCIAL RESPONSIBILITY !

   Oct.
   2002

This chart, drawn by Raymond Ackerman, lists the contributions of four of his mentors to the legs of the four-leg table. They are (1) Gottlieb Duttweiler, founder of the Swiss retail giant Migros (2) Bernardo Trujillo (3) Professor WH Hutt (4) Gustave Ackerman.

Key Statistics – Pick 'n Pay Group

	1967	1977	1987	1994	1997	2000	2001	2002	2003	2004
Turnover (Rm)	–	260.0	2,467.0	6,685.9	9,793.5	13,606.7	15,126.1	18,817.5	26,194.2	29,276.1
Operating profit (Rm)	0.2	7.6	75.7	148.4	190.3	428.0	470.3	622.0	751.2	838.5
Total trading area (000m²)	–	–	268	393	576	679	709	851	935	998
Corporate	20.3	60	268	392	488	492	503	678	748	800
Franchise	–	–	–	1	88	187	206	173	187	198
No of stores	4	40	115	149	362	400	414	471	548	590
Corporate (excl. TM and Auto Centres)	4	40	115	148	237	224	221	332	391	428
Franchise	–	–	–	1	125	176	193	139	157	162
No of employees (000's)	–	5.8	18.9	21.8	25.3	24.7	24.5	27.3	31.0	44.7 *

* From 2004 all part time employees receive full proportionate company benefits and therefore are counted in full as opposed to previously estimating them as one third of a full time employee

The Four Legs

The simple secret that lies at the heart of Pick 'n Pay's success is the fact that the business has grown and prospered balanced squarely on Bernardo Trujillo's model of the Four Legs of the Table, with core values and ethics built into each leg, and with a representative sovereign consumer as the focus of all endeavour.

In the account that follows, I describe major aspects of each of the four legs:

The First Leg: Administration
- Funding (p. 51)
- Managing cash (p. 54)
- Controlling expenses (p. 65)
- Controlling shrinkage (p. 68)
- Ethical corporate governance (p. 75)

The Second Leg: Merchandise
- Consumer sovereignty and successful business practice (p. 91)
- Branding (p. 102)
- Price wars (p. 106)
- Consumer sovereignty and SA food prices (p. 116)

The Third Leg: Promotions/Social Responsibility

- Advertising (p. 124)
- Public relations (p. 128)
- Social responsibility (p. 146)

The Fourth Leg: People

- The soul of a corporation (p. 159)
- Decentralisation (p. 103)
- Investing in people (p. 165)
- Structuring and succession (p. 173)

Although profits certainly are the bloodstream of Pick 'n Pay, making them has never defined our reason for being in business. Profits are the reward, not the reason. The mission statements that have defined Pick 'n Pay's activities since 1967 affirmed our priorities without mention of profits and, as such, they have worked magnificently well: the less attention we paid to profits and the more we gave away, the more the profits piled up – and that is the plain truth.

While the obvious purpose for being in business is to prosper, experience has shown us that the person who starts a new venture and chooses 'making money' as its sole aim is setting it up for failure. As a basic philosophy for running a profitable business, the system of setting a mission and a goal above the prime objective of profit cannot be faulted.

To many observers it may seem utterly implausible that a highly successful business trading in a fiercely competitive climate might genuinely set a goal that ranks higher than maximising profits. But, no matter how cynically one may view a philosophy that places 'giving' above 'getting', and identifies profits as the reward rather than the reason, from our experience one incontrovertible fact emerges: in practice, it works – it just works.

6

The First Leg: Administration

ADMINISTRATION IS TO A business what foundations are to a home. If a home stands on shaky foundations, it does not matter how much love exists within it, how much care and forethought goes into running it. Shaky foundations put everything above them – good, bad and indifferent, past, present and future – at equal risk.

It is perilous in the extreme to ignore or disregard administrative weaknesses. The ability to identify problems when they are still minor, even incipient, and are still containable – a process that can rely as much on intuition as on acumen – is a leadership skill worth its weight in gold in a management structure.

Administration is generally perceived as the least glamorous, the most prosaic leg of the table, yet it is the leg that ensures that the rest of the organisation is able to function.

Administration is generally perceived as the least glamorous, the most prosaic leg of the table, yet it is the leg that ensures that the rest of the organisation is able to function. Adept administrative management in fact determines whether an enterprise will flourish or fail. Inadequately managed, basic elements – such as creditor control, invoice control, expense control, cash management or security – will cause a business to collapse even in the midst, so to speak, of plenty. Mistakes are most often made because fundamentals have been allowed to lapse.

Failures in the First Leg of the Table are most likely to affect the remaining three because, while all four legs must have equal strength and balance, they are, nevertheless, interdependent: what happens under one leg impacts on all. For example, if a retail business lacks cash reserves, it cannot expand and cannot finance refurbishments necessary to prevent the enterprise becoming stale and static, and a commercial world that moves fast is not kind to stagnant enterprises that are unable to keep up. It is to administrators that trail-blazing executives look for the money to widen their horizons.

Brilliant administrators, far from being dull stars in the commercial firmament, need dash, flair and nerves of steel to manage cash reserves that are subject to daily market fluctuations but on whose stability and growth the performance and functions of all four legs rely. Every beneficiary of funds – from executives to employees, suppliers to contractors, bursary students to charities – relies on how well administrators fulfil the obligations of their crucial portfolio.

It is thanks to sound, long-term cash-management strategies in the hands of our administrative people that, when a cash cheque for a sum in excess of R500 million was made out in payment of Pick 'n Pay's 2001 Australian acquisition, those reserves were available and did not place undue strain on the viability of the company's existing interests.

So many small businesses – even some large ones – go down not because there was a shortage of bright ideas or market conditions were wrong or people did not work hard enough, but because – in by far the greatest number of cases – cash flow was not kept positive and insufficient attention was paid to keeping administrative practices sound.

Pick 'n Pay's policies in relation to aspects of administration such as maximising profits (returns on investment) and the management of shrinkage differ markedly from the dictates of conventional business wisdom, as discussion on these topics later in this chapter will show. In the vitally important area of corporate governance, we can claim adherence to ethical principles that predates, by far, current legal requirements.

In the discussion that follows, various aspects of administration are discussed on the assumption that readers will be dipping into these pages in search of the points of difference that have formed the character of Pick 'n Pay, rather than for basic business know-how. The focus, hence, is on the unusual and even unique features on which Pick 'n Pay was built and is sustained.

Funding

Early one morning in 1967, I put my signature to the agreement that I would acquire the small Pick 'n Pay chain for the sum of R620 000. There followed a period of frenzied activity.

The truth was that I had been driven towards agreeing to the asking price because of an absolute conviction that Pick 'n Pay was a business I simply *had* to have. Unfortunately, being unemployed and without large cash reserves at the time, I did not actually have anything like the sum I had agreed to pay. So it was that my brother-in-law Azriel Fine, accountant Harold Gorvy, friend Ivan Lazarus and I swung into action in an attempt to raise the money – with three days in which to do so.

We had offered to settle the asking price as R600 000 in cash and R20 000 in the Raymond Ackerman shares I intended issuing. We thus set about accumulating the required cash through a scheme whereby stakes of R3 000, each made up of R1 500 in capital and R1 500 in loan, were raised from 53 original vendors. Interest on the loan would not be paid for the first two years, making them essentially interest-free. The balance was made up with the entire R100 000 legacy left to me by my recently deceased father and a loan from the Standard Bank, granted after I had presented a balance sheet reflecting every asset my wife and I could name.

Accordingly, Pick 'n Pay changed hands.

As an Ackerman family business, Pick 'n Pay began with the conviction born of past experience that offering consumers merchandise at the lowest possible prices was central to pursuing the aims of consumer sovereignty, already the declared mission of the business.

From the very beginning, the process of buying forward – buying large quantities of items ahead for later release at a lower price, when market prices had risen – was a fundamental policy. The virtues of this system, in so far as the interests of consumers are concerned, is as indisputable today as it was then. However, buying forward and warehousing committed large chunks of cash and impacted heavily on the meagre reserves of the small, young business that we were at the end of the '60s.

Offering lower prices than opposition chains – mainly large, established groups such as Checkers and the OK Bazaars – soon endeared the upstart Pick 'n Pay to Cape Town consumers, and people flooded into our stores. As a result, a hitherto indifferent opposition was alerted to Pick 'n Pay's potential for attracting custom away from them.

Around 18 months later, opposition chains decided among themselves that enough was enough. The gloves came off and a savage price war was unleashed – not to give the public the benefit of rock-bottom prices, but for the sole purpose of sending Pick 'n Pay to the wall. Being bigger and much better funded, these chains could rely on cushioning from a nationwide network that continued to trade profitably while allowing stores in direct competition to Pick 'n Pay in the Cape to trade indefinitely at a loss.

A deadly game of cat and mouse was being played.

Meanwhile, we watched with increasing alarm as our cash reserves began to plummet. What were we to do? Without a national structure to cushion our losses, as our warrior opposition had, how could we drop prices below cost to compete?

Going public

Casting around increasingly desperately for a solution to the first, deadly serious price war unleashed against Pick 'n Pay, we became convinced that our survival depended on outplaying our opposition at their own game. We, too, needed stores that would continue to trade profitably outside the stranglehold of the Cape price-war battleground. We had to force our adversaries to fight on more than one front.

With our very survival at stake, there was no time to be lost.

Recalling a letter I had received from a man who owned a tiny store that he wished to sell, I set off for Port Elizabeth to look the premises over. Although the store in question was truly tiny, intuition at that time of serious crisis told me to buy. Accordingly, I signed a lease securing the Port Elizabeth mini-store and, that very day, a lease over a church hall to boost the meagre space available in the new store.

It was the beginning of Pick 'n Pay's national expansion. We began trading in Port Elizabeth in the Eastern Cape almost immediately and, shortly thereafter, in suburban Johannesburg.

While that early expansion put a stop – though only temporarily, as it turned out – to price-war hostilities, it raised anew the vexed question of funding. Expansion was fine, but it was also expensive and, as a young company, we did so dread borrowing and going deep into debt in order to grow.

When, therefore, my brother Bruce presented us with a case study of Pick 'n Pay going public, devised as part of his postgraduate studies, the brilliance of such a plan was immediately apparent. Why *not* go public when such enormous advantages could be gained? Particularly as we were entitled to apply for a listing as a public company because, although the company in our hands had traded for only one year, the business had been acquired as a running company.

There were also, of course, some disadvantages attached to the plan. A flotation had the potential to provide capital for the growth that was now a fact of our trading life (although we never dreamed expansion would ultimately be on the scale that it has been), but it left us with the question of how to retain family control of Pick 'n Pay.

Lawyer Arnold Galombik, accountant Harold Gorvy and Barney Hoffmann, a man with many bright ideas on issues arising from stock market listings, were called in for consultation and, eventually, a scheme was devised that would allow for a family majority shareholding without compromising the goodwill of potential shareholders. At subsequent meetings with prospective shareholders, the cards were put straight onto the table: in order to retain a majority family shareholding when Pick 'n Pay went public on the Johannesburg Stock Exchange, only a given number of shares would be allocated to prospective buyers.

So it was that on a momentous day in September 1968, amid clamorous scenes at the Diagonal Street headquarters of the Johannesburg Stock Exchange, Pick 'n Pay was listed and, suddenly, became the toast of South Africa. Pick 'n Pay shares, issued at R1,00 and expected to climb to R2,00 on the day, instead shot up to R6,50.

Financial news pages exclaimed in astonishment in big, bold headlines, calling the listing – on a stock exchange not unused at the time to such drama – 'stunning' and 'amazing'.

Post-listing, the concerted attacks by combined opposition supermarket chains continued for a frightening length of time, proving that access to additional funds was indispensable to the welfare and, indeed, continued existence of the company.

In the years since, the company's liquidity has been monitored day by day, month by month, year by year. On the slightest indication that reserves were running lower than we considered comfortable, rights issues – many more than were actually needed – were initiated to attract more shareholder cash.

Managing cash

As Donny Gordon, founder of Liberty Life, once sagely remarked, 'No one ever went broke through having too much cash.'

Having rich cash reserves and the uses to which those reserves are put are key to the success of Pick 'n Pay. A cash-flow plan is as cardinal to the big business as it is to the small or medium enterprise.

As in similar retail businesses, the principle underpinning Pick 'n Pay's existence is that *cash comes in before it has to be paid out*. Cash comes in from every store and outlet seven days a week, every day of the year. It is processed, today, by systems of astonishing sophistication, particularly when compared to the daily calculations relating to stock, expenditure and income we once made on scraps of cardboard.

The way in which Pick 'n Pay invests cash takings (most of which are owed to suppliers for goods that have already been sold) is intended to maximise the contribution of cash to the functioning of the company in the short period before suppliers must be paid. Therefore, the way we choose to invest broadly dictates how we cut the cloth from which the business is fashioned.

The role of rich cash reserves

Pick 'n Pay's policy has always been to have plenty of cash 'in stock', so to speak, in order to be able to do what must be done: buying shares for our staff, financing good bonuses, pursuing the objectives of consumer sovereignty and financing internal and external social responsibility as well as staff welfare.

CASH RESERVES AND THE OTHER LEGS OF THE TABLE

The Second Leg (Merchandise): Should Pick 'n Pay be strapped for cash, we would not have the capacity to buy massive amounts of stock forward, as we do all the time, in order to keep prices down for the benefit of the consumer. Nor could we negotiate those keen, additional discounts – in return for prompt cash settlements to suppliers – that also ultimately reduce prices.

The Third Leg (Promotions/Social Responsibility): It is a simple fact that social responsibility projects cannot be adequately financed without ample cash – without it, we would be unable to respond instantly to urgent need in times of disaster or provide emergency funding to keep desperately needed charitable organisations running when a lack of funds threatens closure.

The Fourth Leg (People): Using cash to buy shares for staff creates enormous incentive for people who would never normally have such an opportunity. Shareholdings foster the sense of having a real stake in the fortunes of the company, which translates directly into improved personal performance and enhanced customer service.

The role of cash reserves has been *absolutely crucial* to the way in which Pick 'n Pay has been built and developed; without them the company would be nowhere near where it is today. The uses to which our cash reserves are put dictate policy and, therefore, impact directly on the day-to-day performance of the company.

Treasury and investments

At its bi-annual meetings, Pick 'n Pay's Treasury Committee carefully plans what will be done with the company's cash reserves and what investments will be made. The Committee is governed by a Treasury Mandate which is of paramount importance in a business such as ours.

As a rule, we have never gone into what are termed 'grey markets' – those markets that offer high interest rates at high risk. Instead, we prefer to make blue-chip investments, and will *never* opt for an extra 1 per cent in interest if it involves any risk *whatsoever.*

Eschewing risk in the company's investment policies is an important point, since it should not be forgotten that a lot of the money being invested is owed to suppliers and manufacturers whose bills must be paid on 35- or 40-day terms of settlement. The Treasury Plan that emerges from meetings of the Treasury Committee is first validated by the Board then scrutinised four times a year to monitor investment decisions and ensure absolute transparency in all Treasury matters.

As pointed out previously, the fact that profits are the bloodstream of Pick 'n Pay does not mean that they define our reason for being in business. Of course we want healthy cash reserves on hand for all the valid reasons already outlined, but the consequence of this is not a compulsion for maximising returns on investment. Pick 'n Pay is not here to maximise *profits*; it is here to maximise *consumer sovereignty.*

Our attitude to market share, which is mainly a Second Leg topic, is mentioned here to make the point that we do not care to plough cash reserves into buying up everything we can just to gain the greatest market share. Our policy is to place quality of performance above quantity of stores.

Gearing

All gearing, or borrowing, whether for start-up funding or any other business purpose, is fraught with hazard. I acquired a strong aversion to debt and a healthy respect for the power of cash by listening to the admonitions of my father, who loathed debt with a passion and could not even bring himself to borrow money to save Ackermans from being taken over.

Although I have a personal aversion to debt and keep in mind the truth that all borrowing is dangerous, having the sense to borrow from time to time in the life of a business is not only necessary but prudent. In fact, a prime cause of failure for new businesses, whether acquired as a going concern or started from scratch, is that there was simply not enough capital to sustain operations.

It is not that the ideas were wrong, the people were inadequate, the time, place or premises or whatever else let the venture down. There was simply not enough cash from the beginning and, subsequently, not enough cash to run day-to-day operations.

I gleaned lessons of vital importance as to how Pick 'n Pay would one day be run from the fate of my father's business – most importantly that, while *judicious* borrowing is an inescapable part of financing a business sensibly, *unmanageable* borrowing (over-gearing) is to be avoided at all costs. As a consequence, Pick 'n Pay has hardly ever geared in all its decades of trading and, as successive results have shown, the company continues to thrive on the broad principle of avoiding excessive debt.

Today, indeed, Pick 'n Pay is commonly criticised for being insufficiently geared: financial consultants constantly advise us to borrow at least half of present equity in order to embark on this or that programme of acquisition.

Postscript to gearing

I have for many years been a member of the Paris-based International Association of Food Chains (CIES), an organisation of retailers representing members whose combined retail trading volume exceeds US$750 billion. I was, indeed, honoured with a term as chairman in 1994/5 and remain eternally grateful for the recognition bestowed on a representative of a trading nation only marginally out of the isolated woods of sanction and reproof, as South Africa was then.

The CIES meets annually at various international venues, and it was at one of these meetings that a fellow member – a retail luminary who ultimately controlled an empire counted collectively as the world's third-largest retail food organisation – made a point of engaging me in debate around gearing strategy. Since heavy borrowing encourages analysts to rate a company up according to the extent to which it is indebted, he believed that Pick 'n Pay ought to set about borrowing heavily against equity in order to embark upon an aggressive programme of acquisition, as he himself was then doing with such astonishing results.

Over years, the more Pick 'n Pay's profits improved, the more he argued his point and the more I dug deeper into my defensive arguments: we wanted cash reserves available to put to uses that seemed, from time to time, to be of immediate benefit to Pick 'n Pay. We did *not want* heavy gearing, did not want to go rampaging around acquiring interests, like so many winner's trophies, just for the sake of it.

The executive who spent so many years waving the enticements of takeovers before my recalcitrant self was the corporate empire-builder Cees van der Hoeven, whose Ahold empire eventually extended across the USA, Latin America, Europe and Asia before it began to unravel amid revelations that expected operating earnings for the fiscal year 2002 had been overstated by an amount that may ultimately prove to be in the region of US$500 million.

At the end of the year 2000, Ahold's net worth amounted to €1.8 billion – on a debt of €2.7 billion; in 2003, Cees van der Hoeven resigned as Ahold's President and Chief Executive Officer.

It took just four dramatic weeks for the solid, impeccably pedigreed company – often prefaced 'Royal' Ahold – that had seemed to have unlimited capital with which to grow through acquisitions, to lose its reputation, its value and its position in core markets. However, present difficulties accepted, I am certain that the flair and aptitude of Cees van der Hoeven will sooner or later guarantee an illustrious return to the centre stage of business.

Takeovers and acquisitions

The business activity at the heart of the Pick 'n Pay Group is the mass retailing of food. Essentially, we are grocers and, although other styles of retailing have been adopted from time to time – franchising, home shopping, in-store expansion of merchandise, financial services – we have chosen not to borrow heavily in order to acquire other assets.

We do not want to buy airlines or health-club empires – nor, indeed, capture every corner of the South African mass food-marketing industry. We choose to utilise and manage our cash in what we believe to be far more productive ways. In fact, when Pick 'n Pay had the opportunity of acquiring two major South African chains, we opted instead to invest the R1.5 billion that would otherwise have been spent on the purchase into an intense programme – part of a 'rebirth' we called Vuselela – designed to refurbish Pick 'n Pay stores countrywide and rejuvenate marketing and people policies.

Until this very day, when members of my own management team are taken with the attractions of acquiring something new, I counsel them to ask very plainly, as I do myself, *Can we really run that business better than the people who are already doing so?*

Personally, I prefer to see Pick 'n Pay as a great *supermarket* chain (a term covering, in the context of our business activities, general merchandise) rather than a great conglomerate trader. All advantage, in the contemporary forum of global trade, does not automatically rest with the great juggernaut empires. At the time of writing, Wal-Mart is the greatest of all supermarket chains.

The bigger and more overcentralised an organisation becomes, the more vulnerable it is to being outmanoeuvred. As destroyers circle a battleship, so smaller, decentralised organisations – being better placed to respond rapidly – have the opportunity, through rapid-response competition, to trim the activities of mega traders and react to the inevitable inefficiencies of big business.

Suppose, for instance, I were to open up a 'Raymond Ackerman' supermarket over the road from Pick 'n Pay's top-performing store at Constantia Village, Cape Town. Because I would be small and unencumbered, I could operate as a destroyer against a battleship. Since the bigger a battleship becomes, the slower it reacts, I could use this to my advantage, setting up rapid-reaction reductions and price advantages before my battleship opponent could even begin to manoeuvre into position in order to retaliate.

Although Pick 'n Pay is extensively decentralised, as a big player in the field we are as vulnerable to becoming a battleship operation as any other large chain. It is vital, therefore, that we, too, stay alert and guard assiduously against inefficiencies.

Property investment

It was Donny Gordon, whose iconic venture Liberty Life, a legendary company started in South Africa in 1957 on a scraped-together capital of R10 000 and valued at more than R30 billion by 1999, who first convinced me that more of Pick 'n Pay's cash reserves ought to go into property.

In 1975, Pick 'n Pay's first Hypermarket at Boksburg, east of Johannesburg, opened to great public acclaim. The enthusiasm with which South African consumers took to hypermarket shopping encouraged us to look towards opening a second development as soon as possible. Hypermarkets, however, are rapacious devourers of capital in developmental stages: the capital investment required to develop, staff and stock one of these lucrative retail giants is truly staggering.

Like the grasshopper economist that I am, always listening for the good counsel of others, I consulted with Donny Gordon, asking him to focus his formidable financial and business brain on where Pick 'n Pay might move in terms of our balance sheet. He concluded that what Pick 'n Pay needed at that time was more substance on our balance sheet, and what could be more immediately substantial than investments in property? He pointed out, astutely and correctly, that potential investors might not be greatly impressed by a new, fairly small company's commitment to consumer sovereignty, but they would be reassured if that same company reflected *substance* (such as property investments) in its balance sheet.

Apart from providing a better inducement for potential investors, owning property – always on the proviso that the cash reserves needed for promoting consumer sovereignty and for our people and social responsibility projects were never depleted – meant that expenditure on rent could be reduced, thus helping to keep in-store prices down. On occasion, too, owning property would give us the freedom to make choices based entirely on the interests of consumers, rather than on the demands of a landlord.

However, although Donny Gordon's property investment advice has worked well for Pick 'n Pay, I cannot say that I have a *huge* enthusiasm for investing in property or, for that matter, much else outside of what I still see as my real vocation – being the grocer at the head of a supermarket chain that pursues the ideals of consumer sovereignty.

Losing property – and gaining loyalty

Apart from sometimes exasperating colleagues who are driven by more commercial imperatives, my attitude towards what I see as my real vocation has at times had unexpected repercussions.

After Pick 'n Pay's first hypermarket opened at Boksburg in 1975, exhausted as we all were following the massive effort that had gone into opening the giant store on time, I knew that I wanted another of these resource-gobbling, demanding, mega-developments as soon as possible. Even, ultimately, a network of them scattered strategically around South Africa. Accordingly, I was constantly on the lookout, ear to the ground, for news of sites that might accommodate hypermarket developments.

Such sites, however, have always been scarce – even in countries such as South Africa and Australia that have an abundance of wide open spaces. When the calculations around demographics, distance and desirability are done, very few sites prove suitable, and competition between retail chains to secure those that do become available has always been keen – cut-throat, in fact, not to put too fine a point to it.

One day in 1976, a delegation of estate agents and lawyers came calling at Pick 'n Pay's Cape Town headquarters. They were offering a potential hypermarket site for sale, one of the last sites close to the major urban areas of Johannesburg that was zoned and suitable for such development. It was rapidly made clear that OK had also expressed an urgent and deep interest in the site in question and so, since both potential purchasers badly wanted to win, bargaining went ahead with verve and determination.

Just when negotiations had reached a critical stage, my secretary interrupted us to tell me that an irate customer insisted on speaking to me on the telephone. Then, as now, it is accepted policy that no person or organisation, no meeting or internal business is more important than a customer. If I am truly unable to take the call, I always call back, but few meetings will be given preference over speaking to a customer – most especially one with a complaint.

On the day in question, my secretary had hesitated before interrupting us, but when she did I immediately excused myself from the avid circle of property negotiators to speak to the caller – a woman who was not satisfied with the quality of the cream cheese she had purchased at a Pick 'n Pay store in Durban.

The conversation around the offending cream cheese went on and on and on. Finally, casting a nervous eye in the direction of the negotiators, I noticed that they were no longer staring irritably in my direction but had begun gathering their papers together: clearly they intended to leave. In a desperate effort to conclude the conversation with the disgruntled customer, I promised I would travel to Natal to deliver personally a basket of replacement cheese to her door just as soon as I could. It was clear from her tone of voice that she did not believe I would really do so, but the offer did terminate a seemingly interminable conversation.

When I was finally able to turn my attention back to the property matter on hand I found, just as I feared, that the cream cheese had cost me the hypermarket site; with another buyer waiting anxiously to take the site, the agents had decided that the petty details of Pick 'n Pay's customer care need no longer detain them.

Years later, when a draft of my biography, *Hearing Grasshoppers Jump*, was under publisher's scrutiny, editors advised leaving out the cream cheese/hypermarket site anecdote, claiming that it stretched their credibility and would certainly affect readers similarly. Was it, after all, really likely that a high-profile businessman would place the value of placating a single customer above a major investment?

The anecdote, accordingly, did not appear, which was a pity because it was in fact true in every detail and illustrates the point that if ideals in business are not *lived*, they simply become a bundle of worthless words.

And what of the lady from Durban whose complaint lost us a valuable hypermarket site?

As I had promised, when I was next in Durban, I delivered a basket of fresh cream cheese to her door, which delighted her greatly. Some time later, I received a list containing over a hundred names, sent by the lady in question, who had persuaded those individuals listed, members of her family and friends and their families, to do their food shopping exclusively with us in future.

So it was that, at the end of the day, a new hypermarket was sacrificed to a few tubs of cream cheese but, since we gained many lifetimes of loyalty, I would say that the end result was a very good trade indeed.

Depreciation

Deciding over what period wasting assets will be written off is a question that all businesses need to consider carefully, and which small businesses should consider even more carefully.

If assets are written off over the full period allowed by the Receiver of Revenue for various asset categories, the depreciation is a lesser charge against profits. If the asset is written off over a shorter time frame, say three or four years, it becomes a larger charge against profits, which consequently reduces profits and therefore the tax due to the Receiver. Having a vested interest in how much tax will ultimately accrue to the Treasury, tax authorities monitor reductions in company profits closely to ensure that such transactions have been managed legitimately.

When I acquired Pick 'n Pay, the company was run according to a conventional 10-year depreciation for fittings and fixtures. Over the intervening years, however, we have tried to advance depreciation periods as a more cautious way of running the business. Although writing off assets more aggressively reduces both profits and tax, it also releases more cash which can be used, in this instance, for the purchase of new and better equipment to provide better service to customers.

Advanced depreciation means that our fixtures are fresh and new and that our stock is cleaner, whereas, if we extended profits to the highest level, we would not have sufficient money to keep our stores pristine. This, in turn, would go against the interests of consumer sovereignty, an important part of which decrees that shoppers should enjoy wide, uncluttered aisles in our stores, the very best in fixtures and fittings, goods and produce displayed in conditions of ultimate suitability for preservation and aesthetic appeal.

Writing assets off as soon as possible – always, of course, within the bounds of what the Receiver allows – in order to release money to buy better equipment is a very good way to run a retail business. We have found over the years that if stores are not refurbished approximately every seven years, sales tend to dip, a fact proven by graph after graph reflecting turnover and sales volumes. Retail outlets that do not keep on renewing ultimately go downhill. In fact, research conducted by Pick 'n Pay has found that customers do not change their shopping alliance from a Pick 'n Pay store that has not been refurbished to another chain; they seek out, rather, a newer Pick 'n Pay outlet at which to shop.

Policy regarding depreciation is not something to leave to an accountant; a wise businessman sits down and thinks it out carefully. Businesses need to constantly review their policy on depreciation to ensure that it obtains maximum benefit for the *specific needs of the company* at specific stages of development.

Controlling expenses

For some time after I acquired Pick 'n Pay, visitors shown into my office would commonly stand at the door looking puzzled as they tried to locate me. Although I would be precisely where the visitor expected to find me – sitting at my desk – I was invisible, hidden completely from view behind the huge pile of cheques I personally scrutinised and signed on a daily basis.

Competent staff were always offering to take this task off my hands, but I had a deep conviction, retained as a principle to this day, that if I did not *personally* watch and know every item and extent of expenditure, I would not truly be in control of the company.

Although this book does not set out to scrutinise the basics of business administration, the virtue and necessity of looking after those basics cannot be overemphasised. In the absence of such close control, a business can neither thrive nor, ultimately, even survive. Growth and stability remain rooted in how well basic administrative functions are carried out.

Controlling expenses pays handsome dividends. Day-to-day expenditure needs to be measured against budget and monitored for warning signs that expenses may be spiralling out of control. Car expenses (including petrol), stationery, salaries and allied matters, such as bonuses linked to productivity and units per man hour, must be assiduously watched.

It is not sufficient to monitor expenses on a monthly basis; it should be done daily and weekly. This is how Pick 'n Pay has been run for nearly 40 years: watching signs such as cash flow, gross margins and profit.

Leading by example and negotiating the best possible terms

That executives in top positions should lead by example in matters pertaining to expense control goes without saying. As Chairman of Pick 'n Pay, I ensure that every cent used on my personal account is noted and repaid. I do not take as much as a paperclip home unless it appears as a debit to my account, and I expect all executives to behave similarly.

If we seem tight or petty about pencils and paperclips, this is part of what allows us to be open-handed and generous in times of dire need, not to mention being able to fund grander policies of social responsibility, black economic empowerment and other commitments of trading in the new South Africa. In the quest to contain and manage expenses, however, we never compromise on quality – false economy goes against the very concept of consumer sovereignty.

Negotiating the best possible terms from *all* service providers, retail and professional, is also a habit that we cultivate. Shortly after I acquired Pick 'n Pay, for instance, we entered into negotiations with Jan Marais, the *enfant terrible* of South African banking in the late 1960s. At the time, Jan Marais and I were a pair well matched. Both mavericks, we were fighting to establish new endeavours that defied the rules and norms governing our markets and our rivals. We set out, with new ideas of service and a total commitment to consumer sovereignty, to set the proverbial cat among South Africa's established commercial pigeons, contentedly cooing in their hide-bound lofts.

Pick 'n Pay had already survived some savage onslaughts from bigger players on the retail food scene. Trust Bank, Jan Marais' young venture, was staring down the banking establishment, defiantly offering prospective clients unheard of concessions, causing the club that then controlled South African banking to splutter in disapproval.

On the conclusion of our negotiations, Trust Bank offered the young Pick 'n Pay a basket brimful of valuable concessions, including one particularly alluring service: the bank was actually prepared to collect cash takings, absolutely free, for an initial five-year period. This was an incredibly valuable concession because, even then, retailers were plagued by cash-in-transit robberies and the cost of safeguarding cash and lives was enormous.

I was impressed, not least because this new bank on the financial block was trading in perfect time to the dictates of consumer sovereignty – this time with Pick 'n Pay in the role of consumer. And, in later years, when Trust Bank was teetering on the brink of collapse and Pick 'n Pay was a pillar Trust Bank client, I was able to repay with loyalty the understanding terms and services the bank proffered when we were relatively small and insignificant.

Mindful of the magnitude of the company's deposits in Trust Bank, Pick 'n Pay's financial directors predictably advised me, somewhat frantically, to authorise the immediate withdrawal of all our cash from the bank when, towards the end of an ordinary trading week, the financial wires suddenly came alive with the news of Trust Bank's imminent demise. Knowing full well that withdrawing our assets would push the bank over the edge, I declined to do so and, instead, spent a dreadful weekend agonising over my decision, tormented by the thought that I might, as my advisors suggested, have gone too far and carried the obligations of loyalty beyond the limits of reason.

Fortunately for Pick 'n Pay's assets, Trust Bank found fresh funding and lived to fight another day, a fact that we used to our benefit from time to time in later contract negotiations with Associated Banks of South Africa (ABSA), the group that ultimately absorbed Trust Bank.

Turnover and expenses

If turnover goes up and expenses are controlled, then percentage expenses to total turnover inevitably go down without any need for penny-pinching.

Pick 'n Pay has always driven strongly for turnover so that, assuming as little as possible is wasted, expenses are reduced. In fact, our overriding aim is to drive for volume *because* that brings expenses down and eliminates the necessity for imposing petty economies.

Units per man hour (or achieving the greatest possible productivity per person) are linked inextricably with the containment of expenses. As a result, we have put enormous effort into working with labour unions so that, today, relations between us are excellent.

Labour unions have helped us achieve greater flexibility by equipping individuals with more than one skill – a process known as multiskilling.

Having the freedom, with the blessing of the unions, to deploy people where they are most needed instead of where their job description decrees, has given the company far greater flexibility in the drive to increase turnover while containing expenses.

When costs happen to go down because turnover has gone up and expenses have been contained, the business is provided with an extra margin, which can either go into profits or be used to reduce prices.

Controlling shrinkage

As all of those who trade will attest, there seems no end to the inventiveness of villains. Whether with shoplifters, or as a result of insider ingenuity, goods leave premises illicitly – from the back door, from the front door, concealed in the most imaginative ways. This problem, named for the *result* of this type of pilferage, is known as 'shrinkage'. It is the scourge of the shopkeeper.

Some of the rackets we have encountered involved concealing stolen goods in vacuum-cleaning bags, buckets of soapy water and even, once, in lumps of unbaked bread dough, resulting in handsome hauls for the perpetrators.

In the case of the rogue bakers, they were admitted to stores by security personnel to work in the early hours of the morning baking fresh bread for the day ahead. At the end of the shift, with racks of fresh bread stacked ready for the store's early-morning shoppers, the bakers, on their way home, were in the habit of throwing lumps of unbaked dough into dustbins to be thrown away because, the bakers explained to security staff, the dough had not risen properly and was therefore useless.

In the quiet of the night, however, they had put the nocturnal lack of in-store security surveillance to good use, plucking a nightly haul of small radios, watches and jewellery off the shelves. As for getting the stolen goods out of the store undetected, well, what could provide a better vehicle than the very tool of their trade – the so-called useless dough that could be retrieved later, hugging the rich haul within?

Another incident I remember well took place in the 1970s, when my elder son, Gareth, was fulfilling his obligation to the two-year military conscription then obligatory for white South African men. One day Gareth telephoned me from his camp in Pretoria in a state of great agitation which, when I heard what had happened, was hardly surprising. Army authorities, for once making a sensible connection between experience and usefulness to the military, had decided that Gareth, who had grown up working with me in the retail food industry, should spend his period of conscription running the large store that supplied army headquarters.

All went well at first – my elder son was, after all, on home ground in a supermarket – until a routine audit of the store's books revealed an accounting shortfall of quite colossal proportions. Grave questions were asked, culminating in the shock announcement that Gareth was to be held responsible for the loss and would face a court martial. When I heard about this sorry state of affairs, I immediately made arrangements to meet my son at a Johannesburg hotel to discuss the crisis. I knew his standards of honesty were impeccable and that the source of the loss was concealed elsewhere – but where, precisely, was the mystery we had to solve.

In Johannesburg, I found Gareth white and shaken, utterly at a loss to explain what could have happened in his store. I thought that the best way to handle the problem was to calmly list every possible way that theft could occur in a supermarket setting. Consequently, large sheets of paper were readied – and I started to write down every iniquity I could recall. At the end of the exercise, I had listed no fewer than 72 ways in which theft could be perpetrated. I handed the list to Gareth, who was already feeling better at the prospect of locating the real culprits, and sent him off back to his store to look into each of the possible explanations.

Meticulous, thorough and driven by a real sense of moral indignation, the wrongly accused Gareth, feeling the weight of an impending court martial heavy on his shoulders, worked through the list of possibilities, his eye returning time and time again to the query I had raised about soft-drink crates, item number 69 on the list. Soft drinks at that time – before the days of canned drinks – were bottled and delivered in heavy wooden crates. The crates themselves were valuable items, billed to suppliers receiving them in the form of a deposit, which was reclaimable on the return of the crates. In large retail outlets, huge numbers of these crates arrived daily and were accordingly debited and credited on their return.

Suddenly possessed of a quiet conviction, Gareth retrieved a mountain of invoices showing soft-drink crate debits – not one of which showed a credit.

What he had uncovered was the work of a syndicate – and there were others working all over South Africa – that relied on insiders to take the valuable crates and claim the deposits. The bigger the retail outlet, the greater the loss – and that was precisely what had been happening at Gareth's store, the discovery of which led to his complete exoneration.

Conventional shrinkage control

When I first ventured into retailing as a young man, in-store procedure decreed that any item of stock lost or damaged had to be marked down in a book especially kept for that purpose. If one bottle of cooking oil was broken, the routine was to run to the book to solemnly enter 'mark-down – 1 bottle of oil'. As simple in nature as this system was, it was not immune to abuse. On the contrary, there was nothing to stop someone recording a mark-down of 100 bottles of oil instead of just one.

When I acquired Pick 'n Pay as a small, going concern in 1967, I looked long and hard at the administrative systems the late Jack Goldin, from whom I had bought the stores, had in place. While I had bought a going concern, this comprised just three small supermarkets and one credit store, so gross margins and the calculation of net profits was a life-or-death proposition, allowing little leeway for error.

However, the more I thought about controlling shrinkage – that crucial component of expense control – the more irrelevant it seemed to worry about *how* shrinkage had actually happened. The components of shrinkage – stealing, mark-downs, breakages and spoilt items – all come down to loss of profit. Whether shrinkage results from theft from the back door, from 'sweethearting' at the tills (the process by which cashiers could charge friends and family less than the marked price, or even nothing at all), wastage or plain bad handling of stock, the result is the same: reduced profits.

The Bradbury/Cohen connection

In the 1960s and '70s, trying to decide on the best way for Pick 'n Pay to handle the question of shrinkage, I approached both Bevan Bradbury, head of Australian supermarket group, Coles, and legendary British retailer Jack Cohen of Tesco to ask if I might look at their chosen methods for controlling shrinkage.

Bradbury told me that he had resolved to cut through all the 'wool', 'fluffing out' – as he saw it – policies aimed at controlling shrinkage in his business. His approach was simple: all he wanted to know, at the end of the day, was how much he had made.

Accordingly, if his gross profit margin was 18 per cent, he presumed 1 per cent for shrinkage and took off expenses at 15 per cent to end with a 2 per cent net profit after taking stock. He did not bother to actually measure the shrinkage percentage – he simply did not care if it comprised known or unknown factors, how store managers had dealt with mark-downs or, indeed, mark-ups; all he cared to know was what percentage he had made at the end.

This unusual approach shocked my conventionally reared retail mind, and I felt decidedly uncomfortable at the prospect of not knowing what was actually happening in our stores: if shrinkage was not measured *at all*, how would a company know if figures were being manipulated?

Then, at some time in the 1970s, I also spoke with Jack Cohen of Tesco. Fixing me with his trademark, no-nonsense gaze, he said that he dealt with shrinkage even more simply than Bradbury in Australia: he just told his store managers that he wanted a zero shrinkage, and how they achieved that was entirely up to them. Any special mark-ups they took, special deals with suppliers, any gains at all could be used to offset shrinkage. Jack Cohen's Tesco managers had a great deal of freedom to choose one course over another – just as long as they achieved the required zero shrinkage.

Pondering these approaches, which differed greatly from the systems on which I had cut my retail teeth, led me to the conclusion that somewhere between the two lay a compromise. Of course, infinitely more sophisticated systems have been established by both Coles and Tesco since the days I first spoke to them, but I nevertheless took heed of their earlier approaches. Through listening and learning at each stage, we have devised a system of shrinkage control at Pick 'n Pay that actively encourages entrepreneurship and has become one of the key factors in our success.

The Pick 'n Pay approach to controlling shrinkage

Prior to price cuts – say, on cooking oil or chickens, for example – existing stock is marked down to meet the campaign 'special' price. Such mark-downs can amount to huge sums and effectively eradicate the gross margin on the goods; marking down a massive amount of stock opens a glaring gap in mark-down figures.

Pick 'n Pay, however, *encourages entrepreneurship* among its managers by allowing them to buy stock above their standard requirements at marked-down prices during special campaigns. When they do so, they know that at the end of the campaign the price of the goods will go back up to their pre-campaign level.

They will therefore have a given amount of stock to mark up, and this is where Pick 'n Pay's administrative policy differs fundamentally from most others. In most companies, the mark-up is put towards gross profit, but in our system, when the price on marked-down goods goes back up, managers are allowed to use that mark-up to offset shrinkage. In this way, Pick 'n Pay allows managers to feel in control of their own domain.

One thing I will say with certainty is that, although the machinations between mark-downs and mark-ups might appear relatively insignificant, in an organisation the size of Pick 'n Pay they make a huge difference to how we do business: the traditional approach says that mark-ups should go to gross profit, but we say that mark-ups should be used to counter all the factors that are against us, whether the result of theft or mark-downs in any form.

In the style of Jack Cohen, Pick 'n Pay managers are also told that we expect a zero shrinkage, but because we know, of course, that a zero shrinkage is entirely unrealistic, our managers are encouraged to negotiate special mark-ups with suppliers to help offset shrinkage.

The Pick 'n Pay system departs from Bevan Bradbury's approach in that *actual* shrinkage is measured half-yearly. Every six months, we ask our store managers: *How far away from a zero shrinkage are you?* With a figure that has been accurately measured, each can be told that they are 0.7, 0.8 or 0.9 per cent away from the ideal zero per cent.

With the reduction of a real figure as a goal, and with the added spurs of inter-store competition and bonuses calculated according to performance in this area, managers have every encouragement to become entrepreneurs in the pursuit of obtaining the best possible deals from suppliers. A manager who is encouraged to make gains in the guise of negotiating a case or two of goods free for his store's birthday celebration, or who obtains a special discount from a supplier in exchange for allocating an 'end' (shelf end), becomes a real trader.

At the end of the day, any assessment of success in the unforgiving world of retail trading comes down to performance figures. As a group, because the combined system of dealing with shrinkage works so well, our *known shrinkage* is measured at well under 1 per cent.

In the early 1990s, the executive of OK Bazaars decided to take the freedom of all negotiation on special small deals away from store managers and, instead, to negotiate all stock deals centrally and distribute from a central warehouse. When there came the hour that the ailing enterprise was deemed beyond ordinary redemption and prospective buyers were looking into its affairs, it was calculated that stopping individual managers from brokering their own small deals had cost OK Bazaars a staggering R55 million – and that without the cost of constructing the central warehouse.

Some R55 million pointlessly lost must have seemed quite a sacrifice when Shoprite Holdings struck a deal to take over the debts of the OK in exchange for a token R1,00.

It must, of course, be acknowledged that the policy of allowing individuals leeway to negotiate special discounts to offset shrinkage does carry with it an increased risk of abuse; there will always be some who become a little too enthusiastic about opportunities for entrepreneurship. But, while no system is perfect and no company can claim to hold all the answers, the system I describe here certainly works efficiently and well within Pick 'n Pay. We have all the evidence of steadily growing profits to prove it.

We continue, meanwhile, to listen for new ideas. Someone, somewhere is bound, sometime, to come up with something better.

'Swell' allowances

Because of the paperwork that would otherwise be generated, we as a company assume – to the ongoing annoyance of both Pick 'n Pay staff and suppliers – that every damaged item came in damaged. This is done openly and honestly and with the compliance of suppliers.

It is common practice for suppliers to give retailers what is called a 'swell' allowance, which is supposed to cover retailers' losses on broken or damaged goods. The trouble is, however, that the calculation for shrinkage (into which damaged goods fall) is around 1 per cent – generally between 1 per cent and 5 per cent – so every time a 'swell' allowance is claimed because this is the route of least effort and inconvenience for both supplier and retailer, some percentage is actually being *lost*. Since Pick 'n Pay makes only 2 per cent after tax, all those lost amounts add up to a lot of money – which can make a critical difference to final calculations of profit.

We simply do not have time to establish precisely how items have become damaged or who exactly was responsible, but we do insist on claiming whatever is lost on damaged items (after the item has been scrutinised by the supplier) rather than taking the easier, but far less satisfactory, route of simply accepting standard 'swell' allowances.

Technology and shrinkage

Fighting on the side of retailers in the never-ending battle to contain shrinkage, modern technology is an ally of incomparable strength and value. For instance, stocks of the 20 items identified as being most vulnerable to theft can be monitored each morning through the use of sophisticated technology. It is then possible to know how many of these items have been sold, how many remain in stock and, therefore, how many have been stolen *each and every day*.

In partnership with technology, is it possible, we wonder, that retailers will one day hold more aces than miscreants in the fight against losses incurred through shrinkage? All we can say is – we most fervently hope so.

Ethical corporate governance

Standing before a Congressional committee in the USA – one of several set up in the year 2002 to investigate various outbreaks of what Alan Greenspan, then Chairman of the Federal Reserve Board of the USA, had identified as an infectious disease named Greed – the chief executive officer of a giant corporation that was about to collapse in great debt and much shame, ended what had been a chilling dialogue with a statement devoid of remorse.

The CEO had been asked whether it had ever occurred to him to use some of the US\$28 million he took with him as a bonus or package of earnings when he resigned from the floundering corporation, to help compensate several thousand employees of his company, who had lost both their jobs and their savings.

'No,' he replied, flatly and unemotionally, 'I'd done my part for the company – I didn't have any further obligation.'

In the face of a multiplicity of similarly remorseless statements from unrepentant executives whose late, great companies fell in upon themselves in a welter of fraud and avarice, taking with them the savings, pensions and livelihoods of thousands of victims, ordinary people everywhere have rightly concluded that personal enrichment at any price has overridden ethical considerations in the conduct of contemporary commerce.

Incorporating corporate social investment issues – environment, health, education, the support of the widest imaginable range of charities and human rights – into contemporary company culture has thus become not only fashionable but essential, especially since analysts now 'mark' companies for share worth according to such commitment and performance.

The concept of the stakeholder

The 'stakeholder' model adopted by Pick 'n Pay in its early days grew out of Trujillo's Four Legs of the Table theory and, in terms of this interpretation, requires maximisation of returns for all stakeholders – the consumer, people, society, supplier and the shareholder – as opposed to the narrow, and potentially dangerous, model that concentrates solely on maximising returns for the shareholder.

However, while a percentage of global business has always adhered to the broader, more humane dictates of 'stakeholder' policy, the 'shareholder' motive has continued to thrive as a dominant force in business, shouldering aside corporate values based on wider humanitarian values. The 'shareholder motive', a dangerous and ruthless philosophy, insists that business exists solely to make money for shareholders. Other stakeholders – employees and their dependants, and communities at large – become merely subsidiary to the main endeavour, which is making money for shareholders.

As such, the 'shareholder' philosophy made massive inroads into boardrooms during the 1980s and 1990s. As early as the 1970s, however, I had been horrified by a comment made by Nobel prize-winning economist Milton Friedman when we dined together with

Anton Rupert, founder of the Rembrandt Group. Friedman maintained that executives who focused on social responsibility were cheating shareholders out of both money and time, which ought rightly to have been spent maximising profits. He reasoned that it was the job of governments, to whom taxes were paid for the purpose, to take care of matters of social responsibility, while business executives took care of piling up the profits.

As a company, we have always taken great issue with this attitude: we believe it is completely wrong. The whole success of Pick 'n Pay is built on the philosophy: *The more you give, the more you get back.* To the cynical observer, this attitude is best read as a good way to build a great business – and who can deny that that is correct? But whether either the cynical or the humanist assessment is accepted, what cannot be denied is that it works – for everyone.

While it is remarkable that so many high-profile companies with apparently unimpeachable credentials have collapsed in the recent past – among them Enron, WorldCom, Ahold and the massive European food group Parmalat – the phenomenon of business failure is actually not new. Companies have always gone down, but latterly, as legislators have scurried to stop the rot of commercial chicanery, corporate governance around the world is being subjected to a scrutiny so remorseless and to regulation so onerous that executives everywhere wonder if it will be possible to continue running their companies at all.

Overreaction is a natural human response, and I am the first to agree, along with all executives of goodwill, that abuse must be curbed. Of course figures may not be falsely inflated or reduced, of course share transaction illegalities, reckless manipulation of monies and other such aberrations must be controlled – but not with measures so Draconian they threaten the very existence of the organisations being disciplined.

New international company legislation, which seeks to establish 'independent' directors upon boards, for instance, runs the very real risk of denying companies the services of the most trusted, experienced and impartial people simply because their association with the company exceeds the number of years arbitrarily deemed to ensure their 'independence'. Lifelong family and financial advisors, past managing directors, the type of valuable advisors I have had on my board for years and years are set to be disqualified by such legislation.

Donny Gordon, now head of Liberty International based in London, responded to the British *Higgs Report* – an enquiry into standards of corporate governance in Britain – by saying that he might just as well appoint the England cricket team to his board, since all candidates of real use to his company are disqualified.

Similarly, and with no wish to be facetious, as I too have to comply with the provisions of new South African company law, I might just as well appoint 12 caddies from my golf club to sit on the board of Pick 'n Pay because they would be, for the time being at least, unquestionably independent.

Share options and the threat of over-reaction to delinquent practice

Provisions of the international General Acceptable Accounting Practices (GAAP) legislation relating to share options, which the South African government intends to adopt, will in future see share options charged against the results of companies. In the case of Pick 'n Pay, we have always *bought* shares to give as options – we have rarely issued new shares to do so.

The giving out of share options in our company culture is hugely important to the maintenance of morale and commitment. People are given batches of shares in appreciation of years and/or excellence of service. What receiving a batch of shares means in the lives of people employed packing shelves or sitting behind a cashier's till is something that has to be seen to be believed – people are *empowered* in the most meaningful ways and, of course, the company reaps enormous benefits in loyalty as a result.

Whatever the reason for awarding share options, whatever the level of the person receiving them or the size of the award, these are shares the company has *bought* in order to *give* to people. They are, therefore, charges against our balance sheet because we have less cash, and consequently less interest on cash, as a result of buying them. According to the provisions of GAAP, promulgated during the 2003 South African financial year and due to be enforced in 2005, shares must be charged as part of salaries although no allowance is made for the fact that shares may perform badly.

If share option legislation is enforced as envisaged, in Pick 'n Pay's case we will be obliged effectively to pay twice for issuing share options. As a consequence, Pick 'n Pay sadly – like a high number of companies in the UK – would have no choice but to review the policy of issuing share options. This would place one of the best avenues of empowerment in jeopardy. Indeed, contemporary legislation on the issue of share options as applied to South African companies goes against some of the soundest fundamentals of black economic empowerment (BEE) policy and is, therefore, self-defeating.

While global concern around delinquent practice in corporate share-dealing is well understood in view of shocking cases of abuse, it certainly seems counterproductive to overreact with the imposition of controls so Draconian that some companies will simply cease to issue share options. When governments complain that too many share options are being given to the top echelon of companies, this is understandable, but when their solutions make it difficult to award shares to *any* class of employee, then overreaction simply becomes counterproductive.

Conducting share transactions ethically

Having discussed what I believe to be an overzealous application of restraint in terms of charging share options, I am *entirely in favour* of rules regulating share transactions that may manipulate the fortunes of companies, whether those trading are non-executive or executive directors. Any such transaction – whether buying or selling – must be preceded by a printed notice in the media and must be reported to the Securities Exchange and that, I believe, *is* good corporate governance.

In Pick 'n Pay we have always adhered to an ethical code where executive share transactions are concerned. None of us is permitted to sell shares without informing a prescribed person. In line with international standards of corporate governance, no share transactions may take place during specified gap periods, for instance after stock-takes and before results announcements.

We have various committees that oversee matters of corporate governance, including the Remunerations Committee, which discusses salaries (including mine), bonuses, share options and so on; the Audit Committee, which is convened to monitor auditing activities; and the Treasury Committee, where decisions are made about investing our funds. They have all been set up to adhere to our own ethical standards rather than to comply with specific legislation.

BEE: Black economic empowerment

Among the thorniest of issues with which post-apartheid business grapples in South Africa are questions arising from government-led initiatives which oblige business to address BEE issues in order to redress disadvantages suffered under apartheid.

At the outset it must be said that Pick 'n Pay is not only working assiduously towards reaching required levels according to the core components listed on the scorecard for broad-based BEE (as all South African companies larger than a defined size are currently required to do), but that as a company we believe absolutely in the rightness and justice of the policy of BEE.

In terms of the requirements of the scorecard, companies are marked on the various components – Equity Ownership, Management, Employment Equity, Skills Development, Preferential Procurement, Enterprise Development, Determination by Sector Enterprise – that make up the content of the scorecard. In our case, I liken the scorecard to matric examination results where different percentages have been awarded for different subjects. Since we implemented policies in some categories – ratios of black staff at middle-management level and skills development, for instance – decades before BEE was even mentioned, our scores are already excellent. In others – percentage of black persons in executive management, for one – there is still work to be done.

At this point, an entire department at Pick 'n Pay, spearheaded by my daughter Suzanne, is working meticulously towards achieving compliance in all categories of our scorecard, and progress is both rapid and excellent.

In striving to comply with present government policies relating to BEE, it is also important to acknowledge past efforts made voluntarily by many South African business leaders in order to redress imbalances. In our case, for instance, 8 per cent of after-tax profits have been poured into all-encompassing social responsibility projects over some 40 years of trading.

Internally, cash reserves have been used to buy shares in the company for all our people with five or more years' service. Millions have been expended on funding education and training, from basic to the highest academic levels, for people both within and without the company. Promotion from within, on merit, started with the appointment of a black store manager, which required a special dispensation from the apartheid government of the 1960s, progressing to the present when over 60 per cent of our store managers are black. Pick 'n Pay also offers one of the best franchise systems in the world, including a training programme for aspirant franchisees, which empowers people to own their own prosperous businesses.

In general, I very much wish that more South African companies would address black economic empowerment issues through similar channels, while acknowledging again the many prominent South African organisations that already do so. The question, however, is this: while the way BEE is currently being organised allows some black people access to South Africa's riches – which is both right and good – surely programmes developed to target large numbers of ordinary South Africans in *real* terms (in this case, our own staff rather than a few wealthy individuals) are the most realistic and *genuinely* helpful tools in the quest towards equalisation?

The question of reparations

Business must put more money into rebuilding South Africa – it is our duty to do so because businesses did, in fact, grow and expand during the apartheid era. This statement, when related to Pick 'n Pay's activities, may surprise many observers who recall that our name was conspicuously absent from the list of subscribers to the reparations initiative organised under the auspices of the National Business Institute (NBI).

The history behind that omission is as follows:

Until its dissolution in the early 1990s, I had been actively involved in the Urban Foundation, established in 1977 as an umbrella beneath which leading figures in South African business raised money, at home and abroad, for social responsibility projects, most notably the provision of housing for the poor. Another important function was the bringing together of business people from different race groups – abnormally separated as we were by apartheid legislation – in order to foster goodwill and understanding and to assist aspirant entrepreneurs wherever possible.

At an inaugural meeting of the Urban Foundation, I suggested that in order to fund the improvement of living conditions in black urban residential areas, a business tithe, worked out either as a percentage on turnover/sales or profits, should be levied on members. The Urban Foundation had itself been started with a tithe levied on sales, and my suggestion was accepted.

Following the dissolution of the Urban Foundation, the NBI was formed in order to help redress inequalities – although, at the time, the initiative was not called reparations, but involved, rather, the duty of the business community of South Africa. Linked to the NBI was the Business Trust (BT), which was charged with funding NBI initiatives. By mid-2003, BT was funded by around R900 million, a goodly pool of capital with which to redress the ravages of apartheid. The initiative, however, attracted almost no funds from the more than one million non-listed businesses in South Africa, nor from hundreds of Johannesburg Securities Exchange (JSE) companies.

When I first came across veteran financial journalist Stephen Mulholland's idea that all companies listed on the JSE should raise their issued share capital by just 1 per cent and pool these shares into a reparations fund, I was immediately impressed by both its sense and its enormous potential. As an indication of that potential, updated to April 2003, 1 per cent of the JSE's capitalisation at that time would have raised R13 billion.

However, at early airings, Mulholland's idea was not well received. Anglo American, for one, argued against the plan, throwing its considerable weight behind the BT model, which it felt would raise more manageable sums.

I did not feel that the 0.2 per cent tithe recommended by the BT was nearly enough, but I was instantly attracted to Stephen Mulholland's plan, particularly as our Board had already elected to allocate a sum of R30 million to a Pick 'n Pay Foundation named the Raymond and Wendy Ackerman Foundation in our honour. Quite by coincidence, it so happened that R30 million at that time *was* 1 per cent of Pick 'n Pay's share capital, so all seemed to fall precisely into place.

Despite the allocation of the R30 million made available by Pick 'n Pay to set up the new foundation tasked with financing enterprises and causes aimed at redressing imbalances in South Africa, the BT continued to insist that we pay the decreed tithe of 0.2 per cent levied on all contributors. This would have amounted to a sum of R6 million over and above the R30 million we had voluntarily put into our own Foundation. In effect, then, we were to be tithed twice as punishment for our generosity – an insistence that seemed breathtakingly unfair. In the end, as a gesture of goodwill, we offered to give the BT a one-off payment of R2 million, but that was coolly refused.

As a result Pick 'n Pay's name did not appear in conjunction with BT reparations initiatives. We retain our association with the NBI, donating well over R100 000 annually towards their efforts, but we are not part of the Business Trust.

The R30-million endowment has not languished in our Raymond and Wendy Ackerman Foundation. Three Pick 'n Pay people are trustees of the Foundation, together with my wife, Wendy, elder son Gareth, and daughter Kathy Robins in their capacities as family trustees. The Foundation continues to do wonderful work entirely as a Pick 'n Pay function.

GOOD CORPORATE GOVERNANCE IN ALL FOUR LEGS

Good corporate governance equals ethics. Fundamentally, good corporate governance comes down – or, rather, reaches up – to high ethical standards in order to attain relevance and dignity. People need to go back to asking: *What is corporate governance if not running an ethical company?* It is because of ethics that we should adopt programmes of social responsibility. It is *ethical*, not politically correct, to pay attention to what happens to the environment and what effect industry has on the conditions all people share.

Helping society with housing, bursaries, medical care or any one of the myriad needs of contemporary community life is not a device designed to garner the approval of the public, the state or the stock market: it is an adherence to our core values and the obligation of ethical corporate governance.

Ethics underlies all four legs of the table that supports Pick 'n Pay, and this was the case long before standards of corporate governance evolved into the issue it is today.

First Leg (Administration)

Ethics in the First Leg of the Table demands behaving as good corporate citizens: that balance sheets are correctly shown; that 'insider' share trading is forbidden; that taxes due to the Receiver are paid timeously; and that tax evasion is outlawed. Ethics in the First Leg demands that executives account as honestly for their own expenditures, however small, as they expect employees to do, and do not see the company as a private fiefdom, a personal cash cow.

Second Leg (Merchandise)

In the Second Leg of the Table, ethics directs efforts against collusion, monopolies, cartels and any authority and circumstance that impacts on the price of food. Although there will always be debate on this subject between different factions, ethics also upholds quality and morality in merchandising. Two examples suffice.

As part of a campaign to stock precisely the goods people wanted on store shelves, questionnaires were sent out to the diplomatic corps in all major South African cities and, in response to demand from francophiles, frogs' legs were sourced from Far Eastern suppliers and placed on Pick 'n Pay shelves. It transpired, on the evidence presented by a delegation of animal rights campaigners, that the cans of frogs' legs stacking the shelves of selected stores were being harvested in conditions of appalling cruelty.

It was clear that a ghastly mistake had been made, quite unwittingly, and had to be rectified at once. All outstanding and future orders for the offending items were rescinded, and all cans taken off the shelves. A considerable donation also went to those campaigning to end the frogs' agony at the hands of unprincipled manufacturers.

On another occasion, I was visited by an angry and affronted customer who placed a horrible little coffin-shaped plastic container, emblazoned with satanic symbols, on my desk. This objectionable object, it turned out, was part of a line of children's stationery on sale in our stores, which included black pens and pencils to go into the 'coffin' pencil box. Such an offensive line should never, of course, have been bought but since it already had, I sent out an immediate countrywide instruction to have the entire line removed from the shelves and sent to my office in Cape Town.

When every last item had been delivered to Cape Town, I arranged to meet the aggrieved customer at a large open field. There, we made a bonfire of every last item and watched them burn away to nothing with great satisfaction.

An ethical conclusion had been reached.

Third Leg (Promotions/Social Responsibility)

In the Third Leg of the Table, ethics means social responsibility: HIV/AIDS programmes and humanitarian aid that disregards religion, colour, creed and political orientation to help alleviate human suffering wherever it happens. In terms of this leg of Pick 'n Pay's table, humanitarian aid is as likely to be sent to suffering civilians in Iraq as it is to flood victims in Mozambique. Ethical governance in the Third Leg builds schools, funds hospitals, provides bursaries and even takes on projects as ambitious as orchestrating an Olympic bid. It also casts a critical eye over advertising, ensuring that it is honest and upright in claims and content.

> ### Fourth Leg (People)
>
> Ethical governance in the Fourth Leg takes care of a company's most precious asset: its people. It ensures better rates of pay, good working conditions, fringe benefits that include housing loans and medical support, and raises spirits through insistence on a policy of upward mobility and recruitment from within. It decrees that people share in company prosperity through the allocation of shares. It acknowledges that employees have families who rely on them, people who are equally affected by what happens in the workplace.

Obvious as it may seem, a document that actually sets out policies of corporate governance within a company is both essential and useful; firstly, company law says you must have one and, secondly, having a written document means that it can be shown to people and the company can be held responsible for implementing its clauses. In essence, however, while words on pages can define the parameters of sound corporate governance, running a demonstrably ethical business is the only course that ultimately counts.

The demonstrable implementation of high ethical standards in corporate governance should form the criteria against which companies are judged. Corporate governance policies, like any other, can be attractive and impressive, lofty pieces of writing – but without honest implementation and belief in their soundness, they lack a beating heart.

At the start, in the middle and at the end of all debate on standards of corporate governance stands one true statement: *Good corporate governance means running a company ethically.*

If executives and leaders, in relation to running any aspect of their enterprise, can answer the question, 'Is this ethical?', in the affirmative, they will know that they are good corporate governors.

First Leg points to remember

- The administrative leg of a business holds the key to the successful functioning of the rest of the organisation.
- Failures in administration are most likely to rebound adversely on the other three legs of the table.
- Rich cash reserves maintain stability and encourage growth in all four legs.
- Strive to achieve quality over quantity.
- Retain a core focus and revisit parameters frequently to assure continuity.
- Watch and know every single item of expenditure.
- Measure day-to-day expenditure against budget and monitor for warning signs indicating that expenses are spiralling out of control.
- Never compromise on quality.
- If turnover goes up and expenses are controlled, then percentage expenses to total turnover inevitably go down – without any need for penny-pinching.
- When expenses go down because turnover has gone up, extra margin is created, which can go towards improving profits or bringing prices down.
- Decentralising business activities brings enormous advantages to all four legs.
- The more you give, the more you get back: there is simply no better way to build a business.
- Set a mission and a goal above the prime objective of making profits.
- Good corporate governance comes down to practising high ethical standards in order to achieve relevance and dignity for all stakeholders.

7

The Second Leg: Merchandise

❝Follow the rallying call *Pile it high and sell it cheap* of pioneer American mass food marketer Clarence Saunders, later taken up as a signature by British Tesco's Jack Cohen. Travel onwards to master-marketer Bernardo Trujillo's definition of modern marketing as *Desirable goods, openly displayed and readily accessible* to arrive at the doors of today's Pick 'n Pay stores.❞

MASS RETAILING, a movement that found purpose and expression in response to need in the USA during the Great Depression, revolutionised the marketing of food. The process saw corner grocer stores evolve into miles of well-stocked supermarket aisles, which in turn started a revolution in distribution. Allied industries such as packaging, refrigeration, store design, display, warehousing and transport came into being in order to service the requirements of an energised food industry that focused on bringing masses of quality merchandise to the public at discounted prices.

Although mass marketing was essentially a phenomenon of the twentieth century, a trailblazing American called Frank Munsey was already extolling the virtues of one-stop shopping as early as 1896, through his Mohican outlets. Retail history has since assumed that Munsey's ventures failed because he was ahead of his time, but it was only 15 years later that Clarence Saunders started selling wholesale groceries for cash only through his Piggly Wiggly stores.

Piggly Wiggly featured the first turnstile checkouts – a point of reference in mass marketing from that time onwards.

As the mass food marketing industry gained confidence in the USA, not everyone watching from the sidelines cheered. A substantial group of old-style traders and their suppliers, backed by legislation and law enforcers, watched the progress of the upstart retailers sourly. When the first retail chains formed, they were furious, mobilising whole communities to fight the invaders on the grounds that the chains destroyed opportunities for young men, practised unfair competition, disorganised distribution and did not save money for consumers – the precise areas in which mass marketing has, ever since, rightly claimed its greatest achievements. In some states, legislation was put in place to curb the expansion of the new chains and, especially in the food industry, there were dark predictions of decline and decay if chain-store activity was permitted to continue unchecked.

American consumers, however, disagreed.

To the chagrin of the disaffected shop-owners, suppliers and officials, consumers confounded the prediction that they would buy less in self-service situations by, in fact, buying more. Consumers soon discovered that they liked deciding what to buy according to clearly marked prices; they were glad to avoid the embarrassment of having to ask a price that they might not be able to afford, and they liked touching goods previously stacked beyond tactile contact. All round, they liked shopping in supermarkets and took to the concept with alacrity – as, eventually, did consumers worldwide.

Significantly, in the early 1930s, the mass retail industry in the USA began to lease factories and warehouses. At these premises of ample proportions foodstuff and household merchandise were sold in previously undreamed-of quantities, piled on trestle tables or make-shift shelves, at discounted prices. Adjacent vacant lots were leased for use as free public parking for patrons, expanding the radius served by the fledgling mega-stores, the forerunners of hypermarkets.

The 1980s Pick 'n Pay Hypermarket jingle – *Pick 'n Pay Hypermarket – Bring your car, you can park it* – reflected a direction that had been defined by the incipient hypermarket outlets of the innovative USA marketers of the '30s. Globally, mass marketing has become infinitely more sophisticated and technology-driven, but certain basics have changed surprisingly little. Acquiring ample parking space as an adjunct to accessibility remains key to planning and maintaining a successful hypermarket venture, and competition between chains vying to acquire suitable large-scale sites has sharpened considerably with the dwindling of urban space.

Apart from obliging a veritable galaxy of satellite industries to improve their products and services, the expansion of mass markets created new roles for both consumers and retailers. As the concept of consumer sovereignty gained credibility, consumers looked to retailers to take up cudgels against price exploitation, manipulation of supplies and other such issues on their behalf.

In the 1950s Mr Schwegman, a grocer from New Orleans, famously chose to go to jail rather than to stop selling milk to the public below the price set by an autocratic Dairy Board. Outraged by this injustice, the public flocked to buy at Mr Schwegman's store to show solidarity with the principles of their champion – an example of enlightened self-interest as trenchant now as it was then. Clearly, consumers look to prominent retailers to champion their cause, and reward those efforts with their loyalty and custom.

The distribution, presentation, preservation and pricing of commodities that the public want to buy, adherence to consumer sovereignty and the moral obligations of retailers are all Second Leg concerns that collectively service the formulae at the heart of mass marketing – keep expenses down, increase volume and, thereby, lower prices.

Cash reserves – a feature of Administration (First Leg) – provide the tools that have enabled Pick 'n Pay to fight the long succession of wars for which we are known and which form part of the Second Leg. Such initiatives, responsible for raising the ire of monopolists, governments and opposition chains alike and for sentencing successive accountants to insomnia as costs were counted, are central to the philosophy on which Pick 'n Pay is built.

How policies relating to commodity wars, food prices, buying ahead on rising markets, the merchandising sense attached to creating islands of loss in seas of profit, negotiating and distribution have become synonymous with the way Pick 'n Pay operates is the crux of our discussion of Merchandise, the Second Leg of our Table.

Consumer sovereignty and successful business practice

The 1963 Modern Merchandising Methods (MMM) conference in McAllen, Texas was marked by an entertaining exchange between conference facilitator Bernardo Trujillo and a British delegate representing Harrods Ltd.

Since opening its doors in 1849, Harrods had become almost too venerable to be called a 'department store', although that, of course, was what it was. It was not surprising, then, that the Harrods representative at the 1963 MMM conference stood up to say, very politely and correctly, that he did not believe that Queen Elizabeth II, the patron whom Harrods served 'By Appointment', would take kindly to the notion of the store pursuing mass marketing techniques. Heaven forbid that shoppers should ever be seen pushing their own trolleys around the hallowed aisles of Harrods in the cause of promoting retail efficiency.

Momentarily checked and clearly puzzled by what he saw as a stunning lack of logic, Bernardo, hands on hips, one eyebrow quizzically raised, enquired of the Harrods executive, 'Tell me, buddy, how many queens do you have?' Trujillo was, of course, nonplussed by the notion that the shopping predilections of one consumer should dictate how countless thousands of her counterparts shopped. The imperatives of mass marketing demanded that masses should be catered for – economic viability required nothing less – and, in the absence of hundreds and thousands of royal customers, the needs of the numerically superior were, surely, supreme.

Next to appear at that morning's royal roll call was the sovereign consumer around whom all modern marketing revolved.

Professor WH Hutt had instilled in my undergraduate mind that it was the responsibility of commerce to serve consumers as people of sovereign importance, standing up relentlessly for their rights, since no one else with any real power would. As a product, and prime proponent of the born-in-the-USA, twentieth-century revolution in mass marketing, Bernardo Trujillo now took Professor Hutt's theories on consumer sovereignty out of their esoteric box, dusted them off and showed precisely how they linked to the practice of marketing as part of a streamlined, profitable enterprise. Bernardo cared about what he believed in – and what he, like Professor Hutt, believed in most was consumer sovereignty.

Among the lessons I learned from Bernardo Trujillo was the virtue of being a good copycat (*Monkey see, monkey do*) and to look carefully at what American retailers – world leaders in the field – were doing before adapting those ideas to our own retail operations. Retailers in South Africa too often persisted in pursuing policies that served their own best interests, those of their suppliers and the government food control boards rather than considering first and foremost what served the best interests of the consumer. Attending those dynamic MMM conferences in the '60s and studying retail trends in the USA showed me ways in which I might steer mass food marketing to new levels of success at home in South Africa to further the cause of consumer sovereignty as part of a profitable business.

Creating a fun atmosphere

I grew up with an acute awareness of the importance of creating exciting trading conditions through watching the way my father introduced event after event into his Ackermans chain. Eventually, his stores were 'on sale' more often than not and he became a master at creating the carnival atmosphere on which retail trade thrives.

I went to the MMM marketing conferences in the USA that so shaped and directed my development as a retail trader already convinced of the magnetic qualities of fun events, especially their potential for creating interest and publicity, generating sales and promoting customer loyalty. It was in the USA that I first saw a '1c Watermelon Day' promotion held in a huge southern county parking lot. A similar event that I organised for the Checkers chain created as much interest among South African consumers.

When I acquired Pick 'n Pay, I also acquired the freedom to use my own judgement to do as I pleased, and I revelled in that freedom. Conservative buyers and cautious board members had been removed from the equation. I decided what was going to happen, I negotiated the deals with suppliers and I took the risk.

Keeping consumer interest alive today is a finely tuned and sophisticated arm of retailing. In essence, however, the ability of a retailer to innovate, to respect the right of consumers to purchase the best quality goods at the best prices in the best environment has not changed at all. It has merely evolved.

Negotiating special discounts

One of the key facets of Pick 'n Pay's policy of promoting consumer sovereignty concerns negotiation – the serious business of achieving the best possible prices and discounts from suppliers in order to pass on the best possible prices to consumers. The practice of negotiating special discounts personifies free enterprise and, at the end of the trading day, it is consumers who benefit. Negotiating special discounts is, therefore, a crucial component in the promotion of consumer sovereignty.

When conducting negotiations, the first point to remember is that the negotiator must be prepared from the outset to lose something: it is simply bad policy to be too keen, because it is then that the fear of losing will place the negotiator at a disadvantage: negotiations conducted too keenly will never be won.

Negotiating is in my blood – I am by nature a trader. When I was personally in charge of conducting negotiations with suppliers, time lost all meaning; there were many occasions on which I kept suppliers late into the night as we wrangled over an odd cent's worth of discount on batches of chickens, for example.

In the early days of my ownership of Pick 'n Pay, I had a secret negotiation weapon – my little black book. With a supplier sitting across the desk from me as I negotiated prices for my few small Pick 'n Pay stores, I would hold my little black book so that the pages were out of sight of the supplier. I would page through and then remind the supplier that, when I was General Manager of Checkers, his company had given such and such a discount to that chain, so why not offer the same to Pick 'n Pay?

The suppliers would, of course, baulk at the outrageous suggestion that minor Pick 'n Pay should have the same discount terms as the mighty Checkers, but they could not help but wonder what telling information was lodged in the pages of my little black book. More often than not, they would grudgingly agree to give Pick 'n Pay the same discounts as Checkers, blissfully unaware that my little black book contained absolutely nothing but blank white pages.

For me, this was a game of poker, a battle of wits between the negotiators at the table. Whatever it was, it was certainly a very effective way to win great discounts for little Pick 'n Pay in its early days.

During negotiations, terms are bandied back and forth between buyers and suppliers. Could we, as buyers, for example, throw in the added incentive of high-yield 'end-shelf' space on store floors? What extra incentive (target discount) can a supplier offer for an exceptionally high purchase? If we reach, say, R1 million in sales, do we receive an additional 1 per cent discount?

Pick 'n Pay's policy of decentralised buying is vital to the entire process of negotiation. Thus, if a national buyer negotiates, for example, a 2 per cent discount with a nationwide supplier, there is nothing to stop a regional buyer from negotiating an additional 1 per cent for a particular region, which gives us, so to speak, two bites of one cherry.

Alleged bad conduct: a war of words

There are many misconceptions about the purposes for which retailers negotiate special discounts and these have, on occasion, led to serious disputes.

On one such occasion, we became embroiled in a war of words with Clive Weil, then the friendly face of Checkers, when he alleged that the system of confidential discounts negotiated between retailers and suppliers were acts of commercial terrorism. Chief among the villains perpetrating these acts, Mr Weil alleged, were Pick 'n Pay's buyers, acting according to company orders. Taking their cue from Checkers, other opposition chains – notably OK Bazaars – gleefully jumped onto this libellous bandwagon, professing equal outrage at our allegedly bad conduct.

This was, of course, an extremely serious allegation because it cast a shadow over perceptions of our integrity. But above all, it was completely untrue. Confidential discounts were termed 'incentives' within our company because they acted as an incentive towards lowering prices for consumers, for which ample proof existed. Confidential discounts, or incentives, certainly did not go into our back pockets, as Mr Weil asserted.

As Pick 'n Pay's lawyers prepared to take legal action against Checkers to force them to withdraw their allegation and apologise publicly, a television station proposed chairing a live debate between Clive Weil and me to thrash out the issue. Somewhat to my surprise, he agreed to appear live with me where, predictably, the talk turned into a clash of titanic proportions. I was determined to extract an apology to re-establish our integrity; Mr Weil, for his part, was equally determined not to give it.

In the end, because I was passionately inflamed by the injustice of the allegations and had evidence to prove my case, I did extract an apology from Clive Weil on live television that night – but the exercise did not turn out entirely in my favour from a public relations point of view.

The trouble was that Clive Weil had established himself as a popular personality. People liked his warmth and friendliness, as well they might, and approved of his lack of pretension – perceptions that Checkers' advertising had deliberately reinforced. When the public saw Mr Weil being humiliated on live television, they felt sorry for him.

Pointing out that Mr Weil would not have had to make the public apology unless he had something for which to apologise was to no avail. Some observers interpreted my passionate insistence as plain bullying and, even though I had been proved right, in the eyes of some I was still wrong.

However, from that time to this, the reason for negotiating special discounts, whatever they are termed, remains crystal clear. It is one of the best possible ways in which savings may be passed onto consumers.

Small suppliers and special discounts

One of the most common accusations levelled against big retail food chains is that large-scale buying and the negotiation of special discounts discriminates unfairly against small suppliers, who cannot sustain price reductions.

Despite popular perceptions, the plain fact is that Pick 'n Pay has always tried to look after the interests of small suppliers. Far predating current government strictures that require retailers to accommodate small independent suppliers, regional Pick 'n Pay offices have, for many years, submitted for my personal scrutiny lists of such suppliers with whom business is being done, complete with details of the price structures under which their goods are being purchased.

It is company policy to try to give small traders an easier ride. Quite often they are paid in cash, or at least within 10 days rather than the usual 40–45 days, and buyers will sometimes avoid or tailor negotiated target discounts.

A small producer's stock – perhaps home-made condiments, jams or delicatessen items – have leading brands as shelf or display neighbours because we know that consumers want this choice. For every small supplier who complains of being unable to place produce on Pick 'n Pay shelves, we have dozens of instances of small suppliers maintaining mutually cordial and beneficial relationships with our regional buyers.

Buying forward on a rising market

It was the indefatigable Bernardo Trujillo who observed that: *No one can be king on a falling market.* When prices are falling, the retail playing field is level. As soon as prices begin to rise, the retailer who can release bought-ahead goods and market them to consumers at lower prices (because the goods were bought forward at lower prices) has a far better chance of becoming 'king'.

Buying forward (buying up large amounts of stock in anticipation of shortage or price increase) is one of the best things retailers can do for consumers. Buying ahead on a rising market is not the exclusive terrain of Pick 'n Pay, but we are the only chain among mass food marketers in South Africa that has consistently pursued this function as a living and active part of company policy, in order to keep prices down for consumers.

Pick 'n Pay's fundamental commitment to buying forward in order to release considerable quantities of a particular commodity at pre-increase prices depends on our having sufficient reserves of cash always available for this purpose.

Buying up massive quantities of stock on a rising market is not a policy for the faint-hearted. It is a gamble and, like any gamble, it can go horribly wrong. Buying ahead also flies in the face of conventional business wisdom – cash tied up in warehouse stock is not, as already noted, cash earning interest.

As a policy, however, buying ahead is an intrinsic part of Pick 'n Pay's policy in the Second Leg. In the beginning, I had to summon up all my courage to take what small cash reserves the company had and put them into large amounts of bought-ahead stock. I remember negotiating with suppliers to buy 10 times the amount of stock my small chain needed when I believed prices were going to rise, but my heart beat crazily as I thought of the implications.

Since then, many talented and diligent company accountants have assumed a haunted look when cash was required to buy ahead, especially when the goods were somewhat unusual. Buying millions of tins of tuna – Pick 'n Pay is one of the retail world's biggest importers of tuna – might not have strained the accountants' credibility too severely, but when cash was requested for buying tons of unsold Christmas merchandise from suppliers in January? The reality of good money tied up for a year in Christmas puddings, mince pies, frostings, baubles and tinsel was extremely difficult to countenance, causing many stolid money men to shake their heads in disbelief.

But consumers, the really important component, have always been very pleased indeed to do some of their Christmas shopping at the previous year's prices.

Warehousing as a factor in buying forward and in pricing

As Pick 'n Pay expanded, special 'buying forward' warehouses (where stock was stored for release when prices had risen) were opened. We did not put down central warehouses because our chain was largely built on direct supplier deliveries to store doors, which obviated the necessity for extensive central warehousing facilities.

The decision to avoid using central warehousing facilities was not the result of a conviction that central warehouses were not the most cost-effective and efficient method of facilitating deliveries to stores. On the contrary, an in-depth survey commissioned by Pick 'n Pay in the 1970s (the first of quite a number) indicated the benefits of central warehousing to both the supplier and the buying chain.

With the results of our first survey to hand, I had approached suppliers with the request that they give Pick 'n Pay enough discount to cover the costs of commissioning a central warehouse and of transporting goods from warehouse to stores. Most suppliers readily agreed to give a little, but the contribution offered was not enough. The decision was thus taken to build stockrooms in every Pick 'n Pay store. We pointed out to suppliers that once these stockrooms were built and the system of delivering to back doors was in place, there could be no change of heart in the direction of implementing central warehousing.

Pick 'n Pay's chief competitors (Checkers and OK Bazaars), in common with most major retailers in the USA and Europe, delivered to their stores from central warehouses. They too, however, had not obtained sufficient funding in the form of special discounts from suppliers and had to absorb steep costs in upkeep and organisation of deliveries from their warehouses. At this stage, as we had committed to receiving deliveries from suppliers direct to our back doors, with warehouses reserved largely for bought-ahead storage, we sometimes had a price advantage over competitors.

Some 10 years ago, with the cooperation of suppliers, Pick 'n Pay put down a central warehouse for perishables in order to ensure that our customers received fresh produce in optimum condition. This meeting halfway between suppliers and the company led to something of a change of heart on the part of suppliers, who now began to express interest in discussing cooperative ventures to extend Pick 'n Pay's central warehousing capacity. Precisely as our surveys had predicted decades ago, it is expensive, time-consuming and inefficient for suppliers to deliver to the back doors of stores, and all of this could have been minimised (to the benefit of consumers) if suppliers had agreed to help fund the central warehousing concept with additional discounts.

Today, this volte-face on the part of suppliers has placed Pick 'n Pay on the horns of a dilemma: we know only too well that deliveries from centralised warehouse facilities are infinitely better for both supplier and recipient, but – just as we once warned would happen – having established our own stockrooms for goods other than bulk bought-forward goods and perishable goods, we have a system in place.

Whichever route is finally decided upon in the great warehousing debate, the interests of consumer sovereignty – getting goods and produce to consumers in optimum condition and at the most competitive price – will remain Pick 'n Pay's priority.

Islands of loss in a sea of profit

From the time local department stores first introduced food sections in the 1950s, there had been intense discussion among South African retailers about the pricing of food as a mass-market commodity.

When the move towards free-standing supermarkets as we know them today started in South Africa, there was still much debate and dissension over calculations of gross margin and profitability.

At the heart of this debate was the fact that department store policy-makers had been schooled to believe that, because expenses were in the region of 30 to 40 per cent, profits on everything had to be at that level.

My love affair with food started in the early 1950s when, as one of a trio of young colleagues, we worked out that if expenses were kept as low as 9 per cent, an 11 or 12 per cent gross margin on fast-moving food could be profitable. While department-store heads continued to toss the perplexing questions of profit margins around their South African boardroom tables, I heard – once again, from Bernardo Trujillo – about a merchandising strategy that created what he called 'islands of loss in a sea of profit'.

Bernardo taught me to position low or even zero per cent mark-up goods – maize and bread, for example – among goods carrying a 3 to 5 per cent margin, fanning out successively to goods with 10, 15 and 20 per cent margins. Thus, remembering that everything sells at a different pace, thousands of chickens, with a 1 per cent profit, might be sold in the 'island of loss zone,' but in the outer circles, where successively less and less is sold, more and more profit might be made.

'Islands of loss in a sea of profit' is a basic Second Leg principle that is applied continuously to merchandising in Pick 'n Pay stores. It is not used merely as a short-term loss-leading measure.

Controlling gross margins

The next step after the successful completion of negotiations between a retail trade buyer and a supplier, when the buyer has bargained long and hard and agreed the very best deal possible, is to decide on a selling price in collaboration with colleagues.

If the product is a fast-moving line – bread, milk or chicken, for instance – then it may be put out at cost (zero per cent mark-up) or at a 1 or 2 per cent mark-up. Gross margin control is inextricably linked with the theory of 'islands of loss in a sea of profit'.

How it is possible for large retailers to manage sales of thousands of items at different margins – some on the slimmest of margins, some even sold at cost – and show an overall profit puzzles many observers.

Imagine the massive amounts of stock bought by Pick 'n Pay today: think of the organisational structure supporting the buying process for 14 hypermarkets, 127 supermarkets, a continuously expanding network of 198 (as at the first quarter of 2004) franchised stores, home shopping facilities and Group Enterprise chains – and then consider the level of sophistication needed to put competitively priced goods on hundreds of thousands of shelves.

While calculating quantities is today part of the science of mass buying, the marvel of modern retailing is technology. The contrast between the scraps of paper I once used to keep track of ordering when I first acquired Pick 'n Pay, and the technology that now monitors every shelf in every store and every region, moment by moment, day by day, is so wide as to be unimaginable.

Overall, retail food chains in South Africa today make in the region of 2 to 3 per cent in pre-tax profit, a small margin compared to the 7 to 9 per cent some chains in the United Kingdom show. To thrive as a mass-market retail organisation demands the backing

- Cost of goods paid to suppliers
- Employees
- Other expenses
- Investors: dividends
- Tax
- After tax profit retained by the business

Added to the enormous challenge of managing different profit margins on different products is the quite staggering range of expenses that must be deducted before any profit can be calculated, as seen above.

of an infinitely organised administrative structure, bolstered by a massive amount of guts.

Although critics will always point accusatory fingers at retailers for the profits we make, there is something much more difficult than showing even the smallest profit.

And that, for food retailers, is showing any profit at all.

Store layout

As part of making our consumers feel at home in our stores, we do not allow ourselves to be swayed by ever more sophisticated scientific analysis relating to layout. Instead, we strive to maintain an environment in which consumers feel 'at home'.

When there is a good reason to move merchandise, great care is taken to inform shoppers about the changes that are about to take place. For bigger stores, printed leaflets detail changed locations, but in all stores, the people I call our 'secret weapons' – customer service managers (our 'Ladies in Red') – are on hand to show customers where they can find what they are looking for.

As a matter of policy, we want consumers to feel as comfortable in our stores as they feel in their own homes. We want our fixtures to be impeccably clean, our trolleys to be pristine and well oiled, our aisles to be wide and uncluttered. The science of why shoppers behave in this way or that is of purely secondary importance to making sure, as a cardinal Second Leg merchandising principle, that customers are as happy among our shelves as they are among the shelves of their own kitchens and pantries.

Branding

When I acquired Pick 'n Pay in 1967, South African retailers had already copied the idea of house brands from their counterparts in the USA. Although Pick 'n Pay's biggest rival chains, OK Bazaars and Checkers, had their own house brands – indeed, I had put those house brands into Checkers myself when I was General Manager there – we decided we wanted something different at Pick 'n Pay.

The No-Name brand

We traded for many years under the slogan *Branded Goods You Know At Prices Really Low* until my son Gareth, then studying in Switzerland, came across a better version of house brands: the no-name concept – a concept that saved much of the expense associated with building a house brand, and most importantly, saved money that would otherwise be spent on the design and production of fancy, full-colour packaging.

Gareth, in a state of great excitement, telephoned me from Switzerland and insisted I fly over immediately so he could show me first-hand the marvellous house brands – products of the Carrefour chain – that had so captivated him. When I saw the Carrefour no-name brand, which was marketed under the slogan *Freedom from High Prices* above a graphic of white doves on the wing, my first excited reaction was: 'I really like this!' Here was an idea that was different from anything else, a no-name brand comprised of top-quality merchandise with peripheral costs cut right to the bone.

I followed Carrefour's brilliant lead and soon Pick 'n Pay's No-Name brand was launched in South Africa. It was a completely new concept, and even improved on existing house brands since, from day one, top quality control went with each and every No-Name product. This emphasis on the quality of the No-Name range is the secret to its success – after all, any fool can sell a product that retails cheaper than a branded item if the quality is inferior.

Of course, many suppliers baulked at the very idea of quality-driven No-Name lines – as indeed they still do today, since for every sale of a No-Name brand one less branded item is sold. Nevertheless, as our buyers point out, support for suppliers' branded items continues in tandem with sales of 'own' or 'house-brand' goods.

South African consumers certainly agreed with our thinking on No-Name goods. Sales burgeoned as the quality-controlled No-Name range of basic food and household products in no-frills packaging went into trolley after trolley – as, indeed, they continue to do.

Seven years after the successful introduction of No-Name brands, it was time for the launch of our next innovation.

Other Pick 'n Pay brands

The Choice range of products was introduced to complement the No-Name range as part of the rebirth that characterised Pick 'n Pay from 1994 onwards. Because Pick 'n Pay's Choice house brand offers customers products that are as good as any leading national brand, but retail generally at a lower price, we tag-lined the idea: *Always the smart choice.*

A unique feature of the Choice range is the 'double your money back' guarantee each product carries. Should a customer not be satisfied with a Choice purchase, double the cost of the product is refunded, a guarantee that I personally endorse. Even higher in quality than No-Name products, Choice products are always placed to the right of a branded item on store shelves and, although it is not always possible, we try to pitch the price of a Choice product slightly lower.

The Foodhall range of Pick 'n Pay products, complementary to the No-Name range, was introduced as part of the extensive changes made to all aspects of the company after 1994. These products are a range of highly perishable, up-market lines that require very special merchandising attention in order to ensure absolutely optimum quality – in each and every outlet, always.

With Pick 'n Pay's range of own brands – No-Name, Choice and Foodhall – requirements and expectations as diverse as our consumers themselves are met at every level, including competitive pricing and impeccable quality. Own brands play a crucial role in ensuring our shelves are stocked with precisely what it is that our consumers want.

Niche marketing

Although the term 'niche marketing' is a relatively recent addition to retail vocabulary, honing in on the products that certain groups of consumers want to see on the shelves of their local Pick 'n Pay has long been a preoccupation of ours.

Many years ago, we set out to talk to people in the foreign embassies in every major South African centre. Out of those conversations came instructions to our buyers – if the French wanted *escargots*, the Greeks *dolmades*, the Japanese sushi, the Americans cranberries and the British pork bangers, then they should readily find those items on the shelves of their local Pick 'n Pay outlet.

Just as certain specialist food retailers in England attract homesick expatriate South Africans to their shops by stocking products like Mrs Ball's chutney and Provita, so we imported full-blooded British favourites such as Robertson's jams, Ambrosia creamed puddings and Branston pickles, among many others, to appeal to British people living in South Africa.

As well as catering to the food foibles of global communities resident in South Africa, niche marketing demands that, for every religious festival and all special days, various dietary laws are complied with – a task that can prove complicated.

I was once surprised to discover that a store that served a large community of Orthodox Jews, adhering scrupulously to the requirements of the Beth Din in relevant departments, was nevertheless not attracting the custom of the local Jewish community. When I asked a rabbi of that community why this was so, he explained that although the store did indeed have a kosher butchery, bakery and delicatessen, strict kosher laws required that an individual, called a *mashgiach*, who was trained according to the Laws of Kashrut, should 'fire up' ('turn on', in modern parlance) the bakery ovens prior to the baking of bread. If ovens were turned on by anyone other than a *mashgiach*, then the process of baking bread according to kosher laws was fatally flawed.

When I instructed managers of kosher departments that in future it was to be a *mashgiach* who switched on the ovens, I could sense on all sides the same unspoken response – the Chairman must have finally gone mad.

Having the required person in store at the dead of night (ovens were turned on at 3 o'clock) to flick the oven switch was obviously going to be an expensive exercise, but if kosher laws required that, it simply had to be done. The point is: if it is our duty as retailers to provide optimum shopping conditions for our entire consumer base, then it is our duty to do so in all respects. Consumer sovereignty demands no less.

Price wars

The landscape we as a company look back on today is strewn with contention: chicken wars, butter-price battles, confrontations with egg, cheese and milk cartels, fish and meat fights. And bread, bread, always bread. I remain steadfast, nevertheless, in the belief that monopolies in any guise are anathema to the principle of consumer sovereignty, a principle that has inevitably led to many difficult encounters over the years.

The first front: bread wars

During the strife-torn '70s, the South African government suddenly announced a rise in the price of bread, an increase of huge import to hundreds of thousands of underprivileged South Africans for whom bread was a staple (and often their only) food.

There was widespread agreement that the insensitive increase would have dreadful ramifications for people who were already deeply impoverished. Even the less-than-sympathetic had to concede that increasing the price of bread was socially inflammable, particularly when the reason for doing so was to protect the interests of bakers, who colluded with government to set the retail bread price.

Collusion between bakers and government was just one aspect of the severe regulatory process to which the production of bread was subject. Bread was regulated – in much the same way as petrol is regulated today – in every aspect, beginning with wheat subsidies for farmers, extending to protection for bakers and ending with the government-decreed price at which retailers were obliged to sell bread.

During the '70s, Pick 'n Pay had put in place a bread subsidy, the first of many over the intervening years, that financed the sale of bread at pre-increase prices into the foreseeable future. At the time, appeals to competitor chains to do the same in the interests of consumers fell on deaf ears. In fact, no other chain would join our initiative, and we were left with no choice but to continue on our own.

One day, during the time that Pick 'n Pay's bread subsidy was in place, I felt a sharp tap on my shoulder as I stood in one of our stores watching the long queues at the bread counter. A solemn-faced civil servant had come to deliver a letter which stated that, in the face of the company's 'defiance', a huge fine would be attached to every loaf Pick 'n Pay sold at the subsidised price, a threat with the potential to bankrupt us in those days.

Sure enough, once the forfeit fine was in place, the amount we 'owed' government climbed crazily higher and higher. Since the public continued to flow gratefully in to buy cheaper bread, we were being pushed – on paper, at least – closer and closer to the abyss of bankruptcy.

At this juncture, the bread price war began to attract the attention of the national media and we experienced renewed proof of the truth of Bernardo Trujillo's oft-repeated aphorism: *Look after consumers, and they will look after you*. People set up such a clamour against the imposition of the fine on Pick 'n Pay that before long the issue became a topic for debate in Parliament.

The outcome of that round in the fight against authoritarian pricing went in our favour. Government was shamed by what the dispute exposed – that they, effectively, preferred to protect wealthy vested interests above those of the poorest of the poor.

In the 1980s, the South African government deregulated the bread price, which created real price competition for the first time. Pick 'n Pay have, ever since, continued to fight one battle after another over bread prices.

Latterly, bread prices merged into the dire South African food-price crisis of the years 2000–2002 when prices spiralled out of control. At that time, with millions more South Africans needing affordable food, tough questions arose about why they could not get it. As inevitably happens when food prices are placed under scrutiny, scapegoats are sought and, of course, the most convenient people to blame, because of their visibility in the food chain, are retailers.

The issue of food prices is discussed further in this chapter in the section on 'Consumer sovereignty and South African food prices'.

Petrol wars: the battle for de-regulation

Whereas most of Pick 'n Pay's commodity wars were fought in short, sharp bursts, our petrol wars have consolidated into an epic with, even today, no cessation of hostilities in sight. The issue at the heart of our ongoing argument with suppliers of petroleum products is simple and unambiguous: their prices are regulated in order to protect the interests of oil companies at the expense of consumers.

When Pick 'n Pay's petrol war proper started in 1975, we had been objecting for some time to the arrogance with which oil companies, under the protection of the law, set prices and cut off any retailer who challenged them. Oil companies purported to control prices to protect the interests of franchised and non-franchised garages trading throughout southern Africa, but it was those very garages that provided the oil companies with their profits and it was, in fact, their own interests they were protecting – again, at the expense of consumers.

A particularly appalling aspect of petrol price control was that each announced increase was accompanied by a deadline. At the stroke of midnight, usually, on the designated date, petrol had to be sold at the new price per litre – regardless of the fact that petrol in storage tanks at the time an increase came into force had been purchased by the garage owner at the pre-increase price. Millions were consequently pocketed every time petrol prices went up, which always seemed to me to be blatant profiteering.

Confronting government and challenging oil companies over petrol pricing is not a task to be taken lightly. The partnership between authority and parties with oil interests has always been powerful and unified. While the oil companies could threaten to cut off supplies, governments could impose heavy fines against retailers selling petrol below gazetted prices, or even close down garages entirely.

In 1975, we began discounting fuel at the 18-pump garage attached to Pick 'n Pay's flagship Boksburg hypermarket. We did so after I managed to persuade our supplier's representative to simply tear out the page that outlawed price cutting in the agreement between us. Fortunately for both of us, the oil company's legal team failed to notice the omission for ages – during which time we quietly continued to discount fuel at our Boksburg pumps.

Once the missing page in the agreement between Trek, our suppliers, and Pick 'n Pay was discovered, a great hue and cry ensued. We, however, refused to be browbeaten by the combined furies of the oil companies and private garage owners primed to support their powerful masters. Instead, we announced our intention to continue selling discounted petrol and went ahead with doing just that.

Despite the wrath of the oil companies and their allies, there was no clarity at that time as to whether petrol price cutting in South Africa was actually illegal or not, and our rebellion stirred the nest of officialdom into a frenzy of action: harried officials, oil executives, civil servants and police milled around in confusion, trying to clarify the legal situation.

Before suppliers, bowing to pressure, were forced to cut off our supplies, the public had formed long queues at the Boksburg pumps, anxious to fill up with discounted fuel. They reacted in jubilation when we successfully challenged a court order served on us banning any further sales of discounted fuel. The court ruled that Trek had committed no crime in selling petrol to us, and we had committed none in buying it.

On that occasion, however, our triumph – a triumph for the right of consumers to buy a product a retailer was prepared to discount – was short-lived. The government acted smartly to close loopholes in the law that had permitted the ruling in our favour, and Round One of the petrol deregulation bout ended in a draw.

The action taken against Pick 'n Pay had been blatantly instigated to protect oil companies and to secure their monopolistic hold on retail sales, thereby guarding against any drop in related government revenues. The situation today has changed depressingly little. Discussion of deregulation of the petrol price continues on its predictable course in South Africa, surviving as a persistent public grumble that grows into a short-lived roar each time a petrol price increase is announced. But even as new stakeholders – suppliers, shareholders and retailers – emerge, consumers continue to be held to ransom over what they pay for petroleum products.

It is claimed that new legislation (the 2003 Petroleum Products Amendment Bill and Petrol Pipeline Bill) is an important move towards a process of gentle deregulation, always measured against the industry's supposed subservience to fluctuations in international oil prices. Meanwhile, government stated in 2003 that it was re-examining arrangements that guarantee a percentage profit for oil companies. There was talk of better checks and balances, and dark warnings of mass unemployment and mayhem among private petrol retailers if deregulation were to proceed too quickly.

When, in the current debate, the regulating authorities continue to state that oil companies are one of the 'best' investors in South Africa, the implication is clear: the interests of the oil companies had better be looked after. Such official sentiments reflect a situation that has fundamentally changed very little since Pick 'n Pay started to fight for deregulation of the oil industry in 1975.

At the time of writing (the latter part of 2004) giving lower prices to South African consumers has been sacrificed to giving businesspeople a chance to buy a stake in the giant oil companies or own their own oil companies under the auspices of Black Economic Empowerment. Petrol prices in South Africa today are still controlled as deeply, or even more deeply, than they were under the pre-1994 government – only this time the person being protected is the black entrepreneur. If it is true to say that one category of person should be protected, then why not apply the same principle to every industry?

However, the debate over entrenched interests is at least being aired more visibly in 2004 than was previously the case. But why should there even be a debate over whose interests are, or should be, paramount? The answer to that question is clear to us at Pick 'n Pay – as clear as it is that the fight for petrol price deregulation is still at Round Eleven in a 12-round bout. The battle, therefore, continues.

Mad Chicken Day (1969)

At least some of the sombre undertones in the commodity and price wars we always seemed to be fighting were lightened by an event that came to be known as 'Mad Chicken Day' – and mad it certainly was.

A very large part of my trading life centred around negotiating the chicken deals that became synonymous with Pick 'n Pay's character as mass food marketers – so much so that I would hardly have known what to do without those chickens. Negotiations with chicken suppliers were tough, ongoing and often protracted and, for me, because of the importance chicken deals had assumed in the conduct of the company's trade, they symbolised what we were trying to do for consumers.

Before Mad Chicken Day, being always on the lookout for ways to put Pick 'n Pay on the retail map, I decided to buy in tens of thousands of chickens, to be put on sale at the pre-metrication, rock-bottom price of 10 cents a pound. The night preceding the sale was a miserable one: I spent it with my wife, my General Manager and several other colleagues, struggling to price mark – with numb, aching fingers – a veritable mountain of slippery, frozen birds. While we dealt with the icy chickens, coming to hate them more and more as the night wore on, we comforted ourselves with thoughts of the many customers the pre-event advertising would bring to the stores next morning.

When the time came to open the stores the next morning, dense crowds had already gathered, blockading entrances in overwhelming numbers, all clamouring to claim their cut-price chicken prizes. Mad Chicken Day advertising had really caught the public imagination and thousands had gathered to form the early queues – some of which were so long they stretched from suburb to suburb.

Press cameras were soon flashing as journalists photographed the frenzy and interviewed members of the crowd of consumers. The

atmosphere was festive from the start, a hive of activity and anticipation – precisely as any good retail event should be.

During the rest of the day the crowds remained good-natured on
the whole. An exception was a slapstick scene when supplies were
running low and one shopper was hit over the head with a disputed
chicken and had to be taken to hospital for stitches. Less combative
consumers were, however, delighted with the idea of Mad Chicken Day
and well pleased with their poultry purchases.

This was just as well because other retailers and chicken suppliers
were anything but delighted. Retailers soon started to accuse suppliers
of unsettling the equilibrium of the industry by selling birds to Pick 'n
Pay at ludicrously low prices – which they had not done. The suppliers
protested their innocence and then, stung by unfounded criticism and
horrified at seeing their carefully price-controlled products on sale at
such unbelievably low prices, rounded on us, threatening to bar further
supplies. If this was how we intended paying back their kindness in
letting us buy their birds in the first place, they said huffily, well, they
just might have to reconsider … the grumbling and recriminations went
on and on.

Meanwhile, the people for whom the entire exercise had been
planned and implemented – our consumers – never forgot the novelty
of the first Mad Chicken Day, which was talked about, in one way or
another, for a long, long time.

Cigarette wars

Another front on which Pick 'n Pay fought for consumers had to
do with the iron rule over cigarette prices once exerted by giant
tobacco interests.

Soon after I acquired Pick 'n Pay, we decided to confront the
tyrannical, price-controlling tobacco giants by buying ahead enough
cigarettes to pack a warehouse full, with the intention of offering
consumers cut-price packs at our stores. In those days, the tobacco
barons dealt swiftly with insubordination, mostly through the simple
expedient of cutting off supplies to rebels who dared to price
cigarettes independently.

While the plan to break the stranglehold of the likes of the United Tobacco Company and the Rembrandt Group was certainly a good one from the point of view of consumers, buying up the necessary stock ahead tied up every cent of capital available in the coffers of fledgling Pick 'n Pay. Nevertheless, the deed had to be done, and so a warehouse was acquired and all available capital reserves were used to pack it full of cigarettes.

When South African insurers subsequently refused to provide cover for what was, after all, the sum total of Pick 'n Pay's capital – our whole life was tied up in those mountains of cigarette cartons – my consternation can only be imagined; if anything untoward were to happen to the warehouse and its precious stock, Pick 'n Pay would come to an untimely end too.

Fire, floods, theft ... disasters too alarming to contemplate threatened our whole existence. In desperation, Pick 'n Pay's chief buyer and I spent anxious nights, pacing up and down the warehouse aisles, nervous and armed to the teeth – a most unlikely pair of security guards.

During the day, my eyes black-ringed from lack of sleep, I continued to petition local insurers to provide cover – but all to no avail. Local insurers were simply not interested in providing cover for what was deemed an unusual, and unusually high, risk.

One morning, a few days into my nocturnal armed-guard activities, a newspaper piece describing the unusual assets insured by Lloyds of London fairly leapt off the page and set me thinking. If Lloyds of London had no problem insuring the finest assets of American movie star Betty Grable (her legs) and Marilyn Monroe's breasts, then why shouldn't they take on my best asset, which at that time happened to be a warehouse full of cigarettes?

Very soon, I was putting this precise point to a Lloyds broker over the telephone. To my vast relief, he agreed that my reasoning was sound and offered just the short-term cover we needed.

Meanwhile, with our stash of cigarettes kept secret, the tobacco barons were completely flummoxed by the fact that Pick 'n Pay continued to sell discounted cigarettes, even though our insubordination had resulted in the manufacturers cutting off our supplies to 'punish' us. Undercover agents were thus tasked with discovering where our mysterious supplies of cigarettes were coming from – real cloak-and-dagger stuff. And, because the war dragged on for so long, our warehouse stocks were eventually exhausted and we had to resort to buying in cigarettes from the unlikeliest sources.

In the thick of the first cut-price cigarette war, Pick 'n Pay issued a press statement that asked why, when we could supply the goods and were happy to do so, we should be prevented from making cheaper cigarettes available to consumers?

The public quite agreed – they did not see why not either.

In the end, after we had made representations to government on numerous occasions, RPM (Resale Price Maintenance) was withdrawn on cigarettes. It was the end of a long-drawn-out and nerve-racking struggle and a triumph for the consumer.

ENLIGHTENED SELF-INTEREST

What I call 'enlightened self-interest' is another of those topics that weave between all Four Legs of the Table. It is a vital part of social responsibility in the Third Leg, but it also influences the Second Leg of our table. The concept of merchandising – policies that govern food prices, subsidies, discounts and the publicity that inevitably surrounds confrontations with authorities over commodity issues – often lends itself to a variety of perceptions, among them the frequently expressed opinion that Pick 'n Pay's public profile on prices and issues is nothing more than a device for boosting sales.

The plain fact is that there has never been a time in my career as a retail trader, a career now spanning over 50 years, when cynical voices from the sidelines have not denounced socially responsible initiatives, in whatever guise they appear, as mere sales gimmicks. Subsidies, discounts, commodity fights and wars with authority, it is argued, act like magnets to draw custom. Even though subsidies are a cost to a company, they still constitute a score in terms of enhancing the company's profile as a socially responsible business – or so the cynical line runs.

Fortunately, listening to Bernardo Trujillo's maxim, *Doing good is good business*, and hearing Swiss retailer Gottlieb Duttweiler explaining his predicament – the more money he gave away, the more flowed back into his Migros empire in the shape of higher profits – provided me with the link, the understanding that running a good business and running a profitable business were indeed compatible.

When discounted merchandise is on offer, chances are good that consumers will want to buy it; in so doing they are exercising their rights, while retailers are doing their duty.

Consider the situation in which we found ourselves in 1975, prior to the opening of our first hypermarket. Certain suppliers objected to having their goods discounted and thus refused to supply the new hypermarket, which compelled us to go to law – unless we wanted the hypermarket to open with certain sections empty of goods. The ensuing confrontation attracted a huge amount of publicity, which in turn attracted the attention of people to what was, after all, a fight for the right of consumers to buy goods that we, as retailers, could make available at discounted prices.

Consumers, like us, did not see why they should be denied discounted prices because a group of suppliers decided to act in concert to limit sales to small retailers, or those chains that agreed not to discount prices.

When the government, bemused by the contradictions and confusions of the Monopolies Act and Resale Price Maintenance legislation then in force, ruled that the recalcitrant suppliers had to allow us to place their goods on the shelves of our Boksburg Hyper, consumers cheered with us and flocked to shop at the Hyper in unprecedented, and sustained, numbers. This was a perfect example of the efficacy of enlightened self-interest: at the end of the day, everyone won, bar the cartel of suppliers bent on unfairly dictating prices and conditions.

Well-publicised fights certainly attract shoppers into stores, but more importantly, they foster loyalty and demonstrate the willingness of a company to live the ideal of promoting consumer sovereignty – rather than just talking about it.

Consumer sovereignty and South African food prices

Food for the people has always been at the heart of politics, and perhaps never more so than during the apartheid era in South Africa. During that time, a plethora of boards directed the fortunes of meat, wheat, maize, deciduous fruit, dairy and most other commodities in order to maintain the price of the produce – not only in the interests of farmers and manufacturers, as they claimed, but also supposedly in the interests of consumers.

As a company infinitely concerned with consumer issues, we began to see during the 1970s and into the early 1980s, how overt control impacted on food prices, especially on basics such as bread, which hit the poorest people hardest. In the 1970s, I personally investigated the effects of cartels, price-fixing, monopolies and the role of manufacturers on the price of basic foodstuffs in South Africa, and presented an 82-page dossier containing my findings to the government of the day.

That dossier was compiled at a time when the price of food locally was rising crazily higher and higher, a situation partly caused – as evidence in my dossier proved – by manufacturers and suppliers jumping onto the bandwagon of metrication, then in the process of being introduced.

Food manufacturers were infuriated by our findings, but they could not deny the accuracy of the evidence that proved their culpability in food-price inflation. Nevertheless, the truth hurt and the resentment stuck.

As a matter of record, Pick 'n Pay received no support from any of South Africa's other big food retailers on the levying of General Sales Tax (GST), now known as Value Added Tax (VAT), on basic foodstuffs to the particular detriment of South Africa's poorest citizens. We originally petitioned Finance Minister Owen Horwood to ask him to balance the plight of the poor against what government coffers gained from GST on basic foodstuffs. As history shows, however, the quest of both retail and consumer-interest groups for a full range of basic necessities zero-rated for tax purposes has been a long and only partially successful one.

A great deal of (unsolicited) publicity has been attracted by food price fights, particularly between government and ourselves, along with our struggle against RPM. This has inevitably fuelled the accusation that Pick 'n Pay – and myself as Chairman – are publicity-seekers, motivated by a desire to promote the business at every, and any, opportunity.

The simple truth is that we did not get involved with any of the issues from which publicity flowed over the years for purposes of self promotion but because, if Pick 'n Pay was to be true to our fundamental goal of fighting for consumer sovereignty, we had no other choice.

Food price regulation in the current situation

If anyone had suggested 10 years ago that I would be arguing today for restrictions on free trade, some red lights to regulate food prices, I would have laughed them out of the room. Raymond Ackerman arguing *against* free trade? A preposterous notion.

I have always argued vehemently in defence of a free enterprise system – what else underpinned Pick 'n Pay's protests against rigid control of commodity prices in the apartheid era? However, as I am obliged to do in the interests of protecting consumer sovereignty, I must speak out against the circumstances now prevailing in South Africa as regards food prices.

Firstly, it is important to point out that I do not advocate government control over the free movement of goods in any way whatsoever. I do believe, however, that the present government needs to put in place some red robots. Of course, many people will contend that restrictions curtail freedom, that they are synonymous with the rigidly controlled society from which South Africa has so lately emerged. I would argue that if you travel down a road and see a red traffic sign that prevents fatal accidents and mayhem, you understand that you are living in a well-regulated society – one that takes preventative measures.

Along with much that is good and positive in the South African economy today, the ANC government is to be commended for listening to the recommendation of Leon Louw, on behalf of the Free Market Foundation, that government do away with the controls on food prices that the previous government had built into a formidable framework of restrictions during a 48-year tenure.

Draconian as the ubiquitous boards of the apartheid era were, however, they did, albeit unconsciously, curb the worst excesses of totally unregulated markets. In fact, since 1994, with all controls removed, the pendulum has swung dangerously far in the opposite direction.

The system of 'parity pricing' must be blamed largely for latter-day increases in the price of food – increases so sharp at times that consumers ran out of notches for tightening their belts. In late 2001, for instance, mielie meal, the staple food of most South Africans, spiralled to an astronomical R45,00 per 12,5 kg bag as a result of a policy that allowed farmers to price maize sold on the local market in US dollars because that is what they would make if their crops were sold on international open markets. In a country like South Africa, which straddles the First and Third worlds, parity pricing is tantamount to 'poverty pricing'.

Certainly, farmers should be eligible for subsidies as relief against the high prices of equipment and machinery bought from overseas. But pricing the produce of their South African fields in dollars? Something has gone abysmally wrong if South Africa has to pay for locally grown maize in US dollars. The free market has been overtaken by a free-for-all.

Meanwhile, I believe that farmers should be supported in the face of natural disasters such as drought, floods, fire and other uncontrollable catastrophes. In such circumstances, government *must* help farmers but farmers, in turn, must help consumers. What will not help any of us – and who is not concerned and affected by food prices? – is apportioning blame for price hikes without seeking fair and equitable solutions.

In 2002, when food prices in South Africa rocketed out of control, a wave of antagonism washed over retailers, ever the scapegoats. This is, perhaps, understandable since it is in retail supermarket outlets that people actually put their hands into their pockets to pay for food purchases. Food stores inevitably have the face of inflation etched on every shelf.

Our reaction to the terrifying events of 2002 was to draw on treasury reserves (the reserves that should be available from sound administrative management in the First Leg) to put a R40-million subsidy in place in order to hold down the price of basic foodstuffs.

Our reaction proved to be a good one, but the question remains – why did food prices spiral out of control in the first place?

Foreign currency markets in 2002 recorded a steady decline in the value of the rand against the US dollar. As the rand fell, so the price of food rose. In the first quarter of 2003, when global terrorism and the impending war in Iraq destabilised international stock and foreign currency markets, the rand staged a remarkable comeback.

Consumers rarely believe retailers when they say prices really are falling, which explains the thinking behind Pick 'n Pay's advertising campaign in late 2003, which compared 2002 prices against lower actual 2003 prices on a range of products.

In mid-2003 a government-created panel was constituted to look into food prices in South Africa. This is by no means an event singular to South Africa; every country has had inquiries into food prices and, contrary to popular belief, retailers are seldom found to be responsible for price hikes.

It is my belief that those charged with investigating food prices in South Africa should look closely at those manufacturers who continuously raise prices. The costs of many raw materials have come way down (those used in the manufacture of cans is a good example) with the strengthening of the currency, but many suppliers simply pocket the windfall. Manufacturers, therefore, need to be asked this direct question: *Are you accounting for the fact that the cost of the raw materials you are bringing in has decreased?* The answer should be quite straightforward.

If any person, or any body, is to get to the bottom of food price inflation in South Africa, they need to ask the right questions of the right people. From a personal point of view, I would be happy to share the knowledge I have accumulated as a result of working for 50 years in South Africa's retail food industry.

Ominously enough, by 2004 there were already calls in government circles for the imposition of set prices in some sectors – a disastrous notion against which I cannot caution too strongly. Fixing food prices would set the stage for renewed supplier tyranny in manipulating price ceilings and would, furthermore, eliminate competition between food chains.

Competition, far from working against the interests of consumer sovereignty, is the ultimate weapon in the scant armoury available to consumers. Pick 'n Pay challenges opposition chains on price on a daily basis, and they challenge us in return. I could certainly have become very comfortable indeed over the years, had I not been obliged to monitor and match and better, where possible, prices charged by opposition chains.

Any notion of setting food prices is diametrically opposed to the basic principles of a free market. Yes, we do need some restraints in a free market in order to protect both farmers and consumers, but we certainly do not need to return to the prison of managed food prices from which we were so recently freed.

Second Leg points to remember

- Furthering consumer sovereignty can be part of a profitable business.
- Consumers look to prominent retailers to champion their cause since no one else with any real power will; consumers reward such efforts with their loyalty and custom.
- The retail trade thrives on the creation of a carnival atmosphere.
- Negotiating special discounts is a crucial component in promoting consumer sovereignty through lower prices.
- He who copies best becomes best.

- No one can be king on a falling market.
- Buying forward is one of the best things a retailer can do for consumers.
- Creating 'islands of loss in a sea of profits' is a basic merchandising principle rather than a short-term loss-leading device.
- Retailers have a duty to provide optimum shopping conditions for their entire consumer base.
- Doing good is good business.
- Monopolies in any guise are anathema to the principle of consumer sovereignty.
- Competition is the ultimate weapon in the scant armoury available to consumers.

8

The Third Leg: Promotions/ Social Responsibility

What happens in the Third Leg of Pick 'n Pay's table gets to the heart of what we believe sets us apart as a retail organisation. In the Third Leg of the Table are some of the most crucial building blocks from which the differences that set Pick 'n Pay apart have been crafted.

All Third Leg activities are joined by a single thread in a common purpose that can be summed up in one sentence: absolutely everything – be it advertising, promotions, communications or social responsibility initiatives – is done to please customers and to enable us to play our role in society.

Sometimes this is obvious. We may launch advertising and sales promotions designed to speak directly to specific groups of customers, flighting 3:00 am radio and television spots for example, for the convenience of Moslem customers preparing for dawn prayers over Ramadan. Less conspicuously, we try to entrench in our people the recognition that they themselves are the Pick 'n Pay brand and that, as such, their contribution to the wellbeing of the company is singular.

Whatever the focus, however, the core purpose of pleasing our customers remains the same.

While many of the projects we adopt require substantial funding – equipping hospitals and building schools, for instance – we ensure that we are also in a position to help with as many small requests as possible. Most requests for assistance are favourably received (even though that assistance may not necessarily be in the form of a cash donation). After all, the people making small requests on behalf of charities, churches, schools and disaster-relief programmes are generally among our valued customers.

As part of our policy of decentralisation (the implications of which will be explored in more detail later in this discussion of the Third Leg), we have set up social responsibility budgets for each region and every store. Pick 'n Pay is, therefore, able to live up to its promise of being 'part of your community' since regional and store managers can address local needs through their own budgets.

Proactively managed, Third Leg activities most clearly demonstrate the interdependence of all Four Legs and the interaction between them. Thus, sound cash management under the First Leg and backbone merchandise policies under the Second help create the funds used in social responsibility programmes under the Third Leg. From policies that fall under the Fourth Leg – People – come the talent, commitment and vision that are key to the implementation of Third Leg social responsibility programmes, which need to be as diverse as the people they serve.

As Chairman of Pick 'n Pay, my view of matters of communication is very personal. Although time constraints mean that consultants are occasionally called upon to outline press releases and announcements, when the media call on me for comment I prefer to address them in my own words and style. All Pick 'n Pay's people, including myself, make an effort to be as available as we possibly can when an interview or comment on an issue is requested by any form of media. Our phone lines and doors are open, but in the event that it is simply not possible to respond to any member of the media immediately, messages are returned at the first opportunity.

Pick 'n Pay's CEO, Sean Summers, has developed a personal relationship with the press and public that follows his own style of management. I was out of the country during the extortion crisis that struck Pick 'n Pay in mid-2003 and vital communications fell mostly to Sean, with the able assistance of Group Marketing Director Jonathan Ackerman, Deputy Chairman David Robins and Retail Division MD Nick Badminton. At the end of the crisis, Sean and his colleagues received well-deserved accolades for their frank and honest management of the unwholesome incident.

Across the world, consumers have come to demand a greater ethical commitment from companies: businesses can no longer just take; they must show a demonstrable concern for employees, customers, the environment and for society as a whole. In 2004, the Johannesburg Securities Exchange introduced a rating for listed South African companies according to their performance in spheres of social responsibility.

We are quietly proud of having lived a policy that predates by far this global sea change in consumer attitude, which now demands higher ethical standards from companies with whom business is transacted.

The 8 per cent after-tax profit that we allocate to social responsibility represents, in many ways, the real soul of the company. Although very few companies, either local or international, allocate a percentage of this magnitude to social-responsibility initiatives, of greater importance than the actual figure is the fact that social responsibility remains a core value of Pick 'n Pay's company culture.

The core values upon which everything at Pick 'n Pay rests are protected through the provisions of legacy documents, to which all with a role to play subscribe wholeheartedly. Financial provisions into the future ensure continued, substantial support for social commitments; humanitarian considerations will always outweigh those relating purely to business.

▨ Advertising

In the early 1930s, when the upstart industry of twentieth-century America – supermarkets – first began to advertise in newspapers, the content and layout of the material they chose was as revolutionary as the industry itself. These pioneering advertisements announced the arrival of a bold new age of marketing, using copy and layouts that were fantastic, unorthodox and quite contrary to what the existing staid and sedate advertising fraternity considered acceptable.

Shockingly expensive full-page spreads bellowed in the boldest black type, 'Price!', 'Price!' and 'Price!' again. The racy language – 'Stupendous', 'Crash', 'Price Fights', 'Price Manglers' – successfully caught the attention of consumers, blaring news of events that impacted on their pockets. People took to heart the carnival air the new American supermarket kings introduced, and went off in satisfactorily large numbers to claim their bargain buys at the discount emporiums.

As for what is today known as 'sales promotions', early American mass retailers simply dragged trestle tables into their no-frills establishments and piled them up with goods 'on promotion'. The promotional displays (offering sale items, demonstrations, tastings and the like) built by today's skilled merchandisers are just more sophisticated versions of trestle tables 'piled high to sell cheap'.

As American consumers became exposed to advertisements that featured their favourite brands at absurdly low prices, Michael Cullen – 'King Kullen' of early American supermarket development – introduced a homely note. He addressed the public personally: 'Who is King Kullen? Is that his right name? Is he this or that? What kind of a man is he?'

'Well, folks, here I am!' his advertisements answered.

With Cullen's intimate approach, the friendly face of neighbour-hood shopping, as a marketing tool, was born and, with the introduction of full-page spreads, boldly worded and built entirely around price, a format was established for mass food advertising that has remained more or less standard to this day.

The evolution of Pick 'n Pay's advertising

When I first met the late David Buirski, then of the advertising agency Hedley Byrne, and tasked him with handling advertising for my new little Pick 'n Pay chain, Julie Green had already been chosen by the agency for the previous owner of Pick 'n Pay to symbolise Mrs Average South Africa. We carried the idea forward and it worked exceptionally well for 25 years.

Pick 'n Pay's advertising and Julie Green became synonymous. Surveys conducted during the years of Julie's 'reign' confirmed time and again that she appealed to an astonishingly broad spectrum of South African women, who identified with her efforts as an ordinary housewife to do the best she could for her family.

Meanwhile, as Pick 'n Pay continued to expand at an astronomical rate throughout the 1970s and '80s, trouble was brewing in the broader world that was apartheid South Africa. In the '80s, in particular, it was difficult indeed for South Africans of all races to look ahead with hope while repressive and ill-advised legislation sparked violently acrimonious reaction inside the country, and the outside world continued to isolate and condemn South Africa.

It was in this climate of bitterness and confusion, with people leaving the country in thousands to become political exiles or to establish new lives as emigrants, that we elected to launch the corporate advertising campaign that recognised and applauded the role ordinary South Africans were playing in keeping the country together.

Here's to the postman, the baker, the learner, the housewife, the nurse ... were the words accompanying images of ordinary South African citizens who, in the face of grave uncertainty and, at times, real physical danger, were simply getting on with their jobs and their lives, providing the backbone services that kept the country running.

Audiences caught the spirit of the 'Here's to' campaign and identified strongly with the characters depicted. We loved the campaign because it expressed our solidarity with the way people were coping and because it echoed the sentiment that kept us moving forward in those dark days – hope in a better future for us all.

In 2004, the *We are getting it right – together* campaign served as an update of the 'Here's to ...' campaign, this time as a celebration of the tenth year of democracy – the triumph that followed the actions and will of all the ordinary people who kept faith in the future during times of great tribulation. This campaign reaffirms our solidarity and commitment both to the people of South Africa and to the nation.

A multiimillion partnership built on a handshake

In line with most retailers, Pick 'n Pay allocates about 1 per cent of sales to advertising. Based on turnovers in the region of R29 billion, this represents one of South Africa's largest ad-spend budgets.

Nearly all our advertising expenditure has remained in the hands of the company I chose shortly after I acquired Pick 'n Pay in 1967. At that time, having come from one of South Africa's largest supermarket chains, I was used to dealing with prominent agencies, but as soon as I met David Buirski and his small company, then called Hedley Byrne, I instinctively knew they were the team to handle advertising for my own small new company.

On the strength of nothing more than a handshake, Young & Rubicam SA (Pty) Limited (which merged with Hedley Byrne) continues to implement an agreement made 37 years ago whereby it devotes the lion's share of its resources to handling Pick 'n Pay's account. In terms of the agreement, Pick 'n Pay does not call for pitches from other agencies and Y&R, in return, lives and breathes Pick 'n Pay, hiring the best creative talent to produce fresh and interesting material – a challenge indeed in the difficult creative climate of retail advertising. For many years, always on the strength of that handshake, Pick 'n Pay was Y&R's sole major client, an example of mutual trust so rare as, possibly, to be unique.

I believe absolutely in the virtue of loyalty as a sound business principle. In all the years I have spent building Pick 'n Pay with my colleagues, the core services of lawyers, accountants, advertising agency and consultants have remained largely unchanged.

It is certainly true to say that when it comes to long-term, mutually beneficial professional relationships based on loyalty, Pick 'n Pay and our reciprocal partners can well claim to be our own best advertisement.

Advertising by not advertising

In the late 1960s and early '70s, we discovered a very useful method of advertising – not to advertise at all. In those days, when such matters were in my own hands, I would select 10 or 15 items (my 'secret items') and I would put them into the stores without any supporting advertising.

Such items, notable among them bridge players' favourite Bicycle playing cards, were deliberately not advertised, firstly so as not to inform opposition chains of special offers they might immediately copy and, secondly, because I took a shrewd guess that like-minded people, talking to each other around, say, a card table, would be bound to mention where playing cards were available at a good price: advertising would thus happen by word of mouth. By the same token, I reasoned that golfers would tell each other where the best-priced golf balls were on sale; that tennis players and table-tennis teams were likely to compare equipment notes, hopefully sending them all to our stores to claim their cut-price prizes.

And I was right.

Encouraged by our early successes, we used similar means to promote various baking items and pieces of equipment – indeed, unadvertised promotions were built around any item we believed might be discussed among like-minded people.

I was personally very pleased by this tactic – and we got away with it for years, having items on sale at the lowest prices, but known as such to those who would want to buy them rather than those who would want to match them.

Public relations

I have never tried consciously to 'build the brand'; what I tried to do was develop the concept of consumer sovereignty and all that that entails. I have never considered myself or Pick 'n Pay brighter than anyone else; we just continue to pick up ideas, travelling overseas regularly and remaining receptive to new initiatives, which we try to implement quickly and incisively.

Accessibility to consumers has been vital in the building of our 'brand', and in the building of our image as the consumer's friend. Consumer sovereignty demands that the consumer – traditionally ignored or disregarded by most governments and big businesses throughout the world – is consistently placed first in every effort on which we embark.

Over the years, considerable publicity has been generated around issues relating to price. Of course, because more people came into our stores, turnover was boosted by our fights to have bread prices cut and released from fixed government control, our campaign to free cigarettes from price control, our efforts to counter the detrimental effects of government boards and the battle we still hope to win on the issue of discounting petrol. More importantly, however, these price-related issues have established a bond between consumers and Pick 'n Pay. This goodwill, a factor beyond value, is a source of enormous pride to us.

Buying goods forward on a rising market, so that a commodity can be offered at pre-rise prices when the general market price has risen, is not considered a form of sales promotion, but as yet another way to endorse consumer sovereignty. We have learned to read markets closely in order to try to pre-empt impending increases, but at times we may decide to fill warehouses with one or another commodity on what is purely an intuitive hunch.

When we have official advance warning that a price – say, of petrol – is going up, prices of existing stock are immediately frozen so that the public need not fear exploitation. There have, however, been occasions on which we have been restrained from allowing our petrol tanks to run dry. At such times, we work out how much money we will be obliged to make on the mark-up of petrol. We then mark down basic items such as bread or chickens to the like amount so that we give back to the public the exact amount we would have made on the petrol mark-up.

In the long battle to achieve discounted petrol, we have tried walking down many promotional avenues – variations on a 'gift with purchase' theme have even been tried – but government always cracks down on such initiatives with depressing rapidity. Nevertheless, we remain undaunted – when one door closes, we make sure that another is soon opened.

Till-slip promotions

Almost 40 years ago, while on a visit to the USA, I came across what struck me as a perfect vehicle for trading with enlightened self-interest. This was a 'till-slip promotion' – in the American instance, for a church that sought to raise funds for the building of a hall in its home town of Dayton, Ohio.

Till-slip promotions – unique to Pick 'n Pay in South Africa – require that customers retain their till slips and submit them to Pick 'n Pay, along with slips collected by helpful family and friends, in exchange for which a cheque is written for a predetermined percentage on the total value of the till slips. If, for example, 1 per cent has been decided on, participants submitting R1 000 000 in till slips will receive a cheque for their cause to the value of R10 000. Deciding what percentage of purchases will be given back in till-slip promotions is done judiciously and carefully.

In the 25 years that Pick 'n Pay has operated till-slip promotions, numerous charities have been assisted, countless schools have equipped themselves with swimming pools, new halls, sports fields and equipment, computer resource centres and so on. Many places of worship of all denominations have also asked to participate in till-slip schemes, and have been accommodated.

Through its till-slip promotions, Pick 'n Pay has been placed just where we wish to be – as 'part of your community'. Personalised initiatives such as these are hugely important to our business.

On countless occasions, adult customers have told me that they shop with us because, when they were children, their parents raised money to put a swimming pool or books or computers into their schools, or because they remembered how a friend had been able to purchase a motorised wheelchair for a disabled child, or because money for something close to their own hearts had been raised through a Pick 'n Pay till-slip promotion.

Affirming core values

In 1994, Pick 'n Pay reached a watershed in its history, following the worst strike the company has known. Apart from causing the company's first ever drop in profits, the strike severely damaged the morale of employees and dented our reputation as leaders in customer courtesy.

New ways forward had to be found. We had to look at the past in order to refocus on doing all the things that had set us apart from our competitors. As part of our journey towards recovery, we initiated a campaign called 'Vuselela' (rebirth) to address, in part, the ills afflicting our people and their relationships with our customers.

We set out to rediscover the core values that made up the guidelines for the way we treated customers. We examined anew how customers were handled at checkouts, whether our people smiled, addressed customers by name where possible, accepted returns graciously and without question – in fact, the very foundation blocks on which Pick 'n Pay had been built.

PICK 'N PAY'S FIVE
UNBREAKABLE
PROMISES

The 'Good to Great' campaign incorporated five unbreakable promises Pick 'n Pay makes to our customers:

1 There will be <u>no queues</u> in our stores, unless all the tills are operating.

2 If we're out of stock of anything, we'll do our best to deliver it to you <u>within 24 hours</u>.

3 Our people will always give you <u>great service</u>.

4 We guarantee that our products will always be <u>absolutely fresh</u>.

5 <u>There will always be a manager</u> at the <u>front of our store</u> to help you.

The two Pick 'n Pay executives who devised the Vuselela campaign – current CEO Sean Summers and then Marketing Director Martin Rosen – embarked on an extended tour through Europe in order to look at the best, most up-to-date and innovative stores on the continent. On their return, a frenzy of rebuilding and refurbishing on a terrifying scale, and costing billions of rands, was set in motion. As an observer, it was difficult not to panic and even more difficult still to keep a cool head as every single Pick 'n Pay store had its insides ripped out for the construction of new interiors, fittings and fixtures.

Since the implementation of the first Vuselela campaign, constant programmes of enhancement have been launched to raise the bar of store operating standards. Vuselela itself has passed through various phases, until, in its present-day incarnation, it was reborn in the guise of our 'Good to Great' campaign, with its slogan of 'excellence 365 days a year'.

Upgrading staff skills, not only through professional training but through a constant process of communication and an active policy of recognising and rewarding outstanding performance or commitment, has meant that campaigns such as 'Good to Great' have been taken to heart. Our customers are the ultimate winners.

The core purpose of the 'Good to Great' initiative and other innovative sales promotion ideas is to take the company to the point where, should some giant of the retail world – a Wal-Mart, say – decide to open up in South Africa, it will find itself faced with a local competitor that operates according to the highest standards in the world.

Living public relations

In Pick 'n Pay, we have a saying: 'We do not buy public relations – we live them.' This means that public relations is a living discipline, practised on all levels as an intrinsic part of our company culture rather than according to textbook norms and conventional strategies.

All visitors, including suppliers and sales representatives, are treated with courtesy and consideration, offered tea while they wait or something to eat if it is lunch time, because every visitor to our

---

BANDANA DAY: AN EXAMPLE OF CORE VALUES

The 2003 Bandana Day fund-raising drive, an initiative on behalf of the Sunflower Fund, which supports leukaemia sufferers and promotes life-saving bone-marrow transplantation, is an excellent annual example of a commitment to core values that filters through every part of the company.

The basic fund-raising drive of the campaign is the sale, at Pick 'n Pay outlets, of bandanas, signifying solidarity with leukaemia patients who have suffered hair loss as a result of chemotherapy treatment.

Pick 'n Pay people put their hearts into raising levels of public aware-ness around the issue of bone-marrow transplants, and senior Pick 'n Pay executives as well as many managers up and down the country took the lead and shaved their heads as a mark of solidarity with sufferers.

Bandana Day 2003 raised the handsome sum of R1.4 million for the Sunflower Fund. How much Pick 'n Pay is a part of the local communities was reaffirmed when, following our lead, police, flight staff, school children, banks, staff of other retailers, dogs and horses all wore bandanas in solidarity with the cause.

---

offices is a potential customer. A supplier who has come in to promote his company's wares is also a consumer, with a family and friends who are consumers too.

Practising basic courtesy, showing simple good manners, is living public relations, as are our efforts to please the customer by providing the best shopping environment we can.

Giving time

In promoting and cementing good public relations, time is worth far more than money.

While there is no doubt that public-relations professionals are indispensable to the smooth running of modern commerce, company executives themselves should always invest time in staying in touch with the public. Public speaking is regarded as very important in this regard and all our executives make themselves available for speaking engagements. In my own case, I give two to three speeches every week when I am in South Africa.

SIX DAYS IN THE LIFE OF PICK 'N PAY

Saturday, 18 May 2004: Zurich, Switzerland – 2010 World Cup Soccer Announcement

In Zurich, Pick 'n Pay CEO Sean Summers and Director Isaac Motaung linked arms with a line of jubilant South African luminaries – among them, President Thabo Mbeki, ex-presidents Nelson Mandela and FW de Klerk, Archbishop Emeritus Desmond Tutu and bid leader Danny Jordaan – to share the sheer joy of hearing that South Africa had won the right to host the 2010 Soccer World Cup.

As sponsors of the 2010 Soccer World Cup, having our name visible at the Zurich announcement ceremony may have been sufficient. As it was, when Sean Summers and Isaac Motaung travelled all the way to Zurich to show solidarity with South Africa's bid, when they joined arms and cheered our country's triumph with the leaders and personalities closest to the hearts of South Africa's people, they were living public relations for Pick 'n Pay.

As host to this major event, the South African government's scorecard for 2010 will contain such projects as improving public transport and making it safe; showcasing the country's humanity by replacing as many shacks as possible with low-cost houses; and clearing up crime. Government has a deadline, an 'examination date' if you like, by which time all must be done and ready.

Sunday, 19 May 2004: Table Mountain, Cape Town – The Tastic Table of Unity

Past history has shown us the power of sporting events to iron out the creases of diversity in the fabric of South African lives. It was thus fitting that the day following the triumphal announcement of the 2010 Soccer Cup coup was designated 'South African Day of Peace and Unity', to be celebrated around the Tastic Table of Unity at the top of Table Mountain.

Our General Manager of Corporate Affairs, Suzanne Ackerman, was part of this annual event catered by Pick 'n Pay, at which hundreds are seated around the 'Tastic Table' to promote peace and goodwill among the people of South Africa.

Participation in the occasion is an event into which we put our whole heart; the principles of the initiative resonate deeply with us for the way in which the sharing of a meal by people of widely differing backgrounds signifies the giant steps South Africans have taken towards unity in our diversity.

Monday, 20 March 2004: 'READ' and the quest to enable learners (Riviersonderend)

On the morning of Monday, 20 March, Pick 'n Pay Deputy Chairman David Robins, Llewellyn Dyer, General Manager Cape, and Bakar Jakoet, Retail Financial Director, settled down to evaluate the results of the very long, very hard weekend they had spent, with their families, driving around painfully inaccessible rural areas to deliver books to extremely under-privileged people, under the auspices of the READ initiative.

Studies undertaken by READ among South Africa's school-going population suggest that the core reason for failing grades or simply dropping out of school is the lack of basic learning skills, most crucially a lack of adequate language skills. The READ Educational Trust, a non-profit organisation, seeks to remedy this situation through various means, chiefly by improving access to reading material.

Much of Pick 'n Pay's social responsibility is effected in the company's name, but we frequently ally ourselves with other organisations and charities where this facilitates efficiency – the fastest way to give people what they need is the name of this particular game. READ has received our support for many years, because we passionately believe in its objectives.

Wednesday, 22 March 2004: Assessing the Disney Institute's 'Build the Brand' programme

By the afternoon of Wednesday, 22 March 2004, Pick 'n Pay Marketing Director Jonathan Ackerman, Retail Division Managing Director Nic Badminton and their team were assessing the progress of the current group of Pick 'n Pay achievers attending the Disney Service Standards programme 'Build the Brand' at the Disney Institute.

This post-1994 initiative is a reward and incentive for staff who show a singular commitment to the company's pursuit of consumer sovereignty. Participating staff learn from the masters the finest points and the purpose of courtesy, bringing back a legacy of knowledge to share with their colleagues – a prime example of how Third Leg principles dedicated to serving customers impeccably are best communicated from person to committed person.

Those who have attended the Disney Institute have since, through putting into practice in the workplace at home what they learned at Disney, helped to reinforce the notion that employees themselves are the Pick 'n Pay brand. It is they who make the most significant difference to public perceptions by living public relations.

Thursday, 23 March 2004: Khayelitsha, Cape Town 'Habitat for Humanity' Project

Recognising the value of Habitat for Humanity's vision of 'a world where everyone has a decent place to live', we as a company have lent all the support we can to this worthwhile cause. Pick 'n Pay and the people of Habitat for Humanity had cooperated closely on many occasions, well before the Thursday afternoon when the Chairman and his wife made their own personal contribution to living public relations by becoming builders for a day.

Habitat for Humanity, a non-profit Christian organisation dedicated to making the provision of adequate, affordable shelter a matter of conscience and action, is not a charity, but a partnership. Instead of giving away houses, it helps homeowners to build their own houses and those of others, working alongside volunteers. Ultimately, homeowners repay the cost of their houses by paying off a non-profit, interest-free loan.

The provision of decent housing for our people, and the financing thereof, has preoccupied our company for decades. Schemes whereby Pick 'n Pay people are empowered to own their own houses are a crucial part of staff benefits.

Friday, 24 March 2004: Constantia, Cape Town – The Wheat Trust

When 1 000 women arrived at a lunch hosted by Pick 'n Pay Executive Board Member, Wendy Ackerman, the objective went beyond fund-raising for the Wheat (Women's Hope Education and Training) Trust. The cause of empowering South African women goes to the heart of how Pick 'n Pay, as a company, sees the future of our country, how we believe we can all grow in strength and compassion and gain a greater sense of community.

In order to empower women to uplift their communities, the Wheat Trust sets out to provide the necessary mechanisms, an initiative they have named 'Dreams to Grow'. Presently, of the approximately 50 000 projects led by women in South Africa, the overwhelming majority have no funding at all.

An anecdote that always pleases audiences at my many speaking engagements in the course of the year relates to the broad issue of public relations and how time is indeed worth more than money.

Many years ago, the car in which I was travelling in Cape Town pulled up next to a laden station wagon at a red traffic light. At the very moment that the signal turned from red to green and the station wagon shot forward, I saw from the goodly pile of supermarket bags in the back of the vehicle that the driver was returning from a big shopping expedition – at a Checkers store, as the pile of yellow bags revealed.

'Follow that car!' I told my startled driver. 'Follow it wherever it goes', and off we set in pursuit. Weaving in and out of morning traffic, craning to keep the station wagon in sight, we followed it all the way to the suburb of Fish Hoek, where the woman pulled into the driveway of her home and began unloading her Checkers bags.

Suddenly feeling quite silly about what I had done, yet nevertheless intrigued, I approached her and, with apologies for the intrusion, asked her if she would mind telling me why she shopped at Checkers and not at Pick 'n Pay? Had we done something to upset her?

'Yes,' she replied, 'you have.'

It transpired that some years previously she had been treated rudely by a cashier who had argued about some item she had wished to return. We had tea and talked it over, I offered an apology and told her that a cornerstone of Pick 'n Pay's customer-service policy is to accept goods back graciously. She was very pleased to have someone listen to her long-held grievance and to have received the apology she deserved. By the time we parted, all was well. She promised to give us another chance to make good on our previous error, and I went away confident that she might become a loyal customer again.

At base, it had been more than a simple case of trader's curiosity that made me want to find out why that consumer chose to shop with a competitor: if we were wrong, I wanted to know why.

Giving time has as much value in creating loyalty and building relations as cash given in the form of a donation. This emerges from the many warm stories I am told, often at public speaking engagements: an elderly man who remembers being offered a cup of tea when he came to audit our books as a young clerk starting out on his career; grandmothers recalling a time 30 years before, when they came to see us about raising money to build a classroom at their children's school; grandchildren who profited from such ventures. Generations may follow a family tradition of shopping with us because a grandmother received a donation to her favourite charity as a girl or a relation received some help when the family was in crisis.

The point is, people remember the smallest amount of attention or seemingly insignificant effort if it is offered with genuine warmth, and the likelihood is that, in return, they will shop with you for the rest of their lives. The ripple effect of small public-relations gestures spreads unexpectedly far.

It is precisely in this light that Pick 'n Pay has supported university Rag appeals throughout the country, and we have a particularly warm and enduring relationship with the University of Cape Town's annual Rag appeal. Our involvement at UCT and other South African tertiary institutions, through funding for the institutions and study bursaries for numerous students, has a very serious side. While we identify with the fun and youthful exuberance that characterises Rag, we recognise the importance of the fund raising that is its purpose.

Being involved with young people at this level is a remarkably effective way of getting them on your side, and it is equally amazing how they will stay with you all their lives if they are not sent away with the stock answer of 'Sorry, our budget is full', when they come knocking at your door in search of funds. For years, before such harmless fun became politically incorrect, the UCT Rag Queen elections were held under a huge banner emblazoned *You Pick your Queen, now Pay.*

There is hardly a page among the mountain of diaries that have regulated my business life that does not have time allocated to meeting people whose lives have taken unexpected turns for the worse and who are consequently in search of a new direction. Through these appointments, I sometimes discover absolute gems, people whose courage and fortitude humbles me, but I also glean incredibly useful first-hand information about public perceptions of Pick 'n Pay – where we are right, where we are wrong, and where we need to do better.

Ladies in Red

I first saw consumer advisors at work in the Giant Supermarket chain in the USA. Giant's first such person had been no less than a Minister of Consumer Affairs. The Giant Group had employed her to fulfil the same role within their chain of stores, creating their own team of consumer advisors called 'Ladies in Red'.

As a result of seeing what Giant had done, Pick 'n Pay's Customer Service Managers came into being. Since then, competing South African chains have tried introducing their own consumer advisory services, but none have persisted with the idea. In fact, the successor to the great Jack Cohen of Tesco, England, was once greatly taken with the idea of employing consumer advisors after seeing Pick 'n Pay's Ladies in Red at work. He resolved to introduce a similar service for Tesco customers and did so for a short time, but did not persist with the idea.

Today, our Customer Service Managers are absolutely critical to the running of our stores. Every store has one or two, and big stores even three or four. Our Ladies in Red play a very important role in liaising with customers. They get to know individual customers, particularly those with special needs, and promote goodwill between stores and local communities.

Should a visually handicapped person, for instance, need help in one of our stores, a Lady in Red not only offers assistance, but establishes a friendly and caring relationship with the customer. In some areas, special transport is arranged to bring groups of pensioners from old-age homes to do their shopping at a convenient Pick 'n Pay store, and again it is the local Ladies in Red who host the visitors and facilitate their shopping.

Customer care that goes far beyond what might be ordinarily expected is a fine example for all Pick 'n Pay's people. We came to hear, for instance, of a young person employed as a checkout assistant at our Sea Point store who had taken it upon himself to personally shop for an elderly pensioner he had come to know at the store. He was taking the shopping to the pensioner's house, unpacking it into her cupboards, doing household chores that obviously could not be managed, then returning in the evenings after work to read to the poorly sighted pensioner.

Pick 'n Pay stores across South Africa are involved in dozens of local social responsibility projects. Customer Service Managers petition divisional General Managers for funds to assist with local initiatives. Not only does this do an enormous amount of good, it also forges and maintains solid ties with local communities.

Our Ladies in Red all keep a 'brag' book detailing what they have done month by month; there is intense rivalry among them to achieve the most in terms of the depth and range of initiatives with which they are involved.

Considering the unbelievable amount of detailed social responsibility work that is being done throughout the country, and considering the vitally important personal, lasting relationships fostered with individual Pick 'n Pay customers through our Customer Service Managers, it is no wonder that we call them our 'secret weapon'.

Crisis management

In 2003, an anonymous male caller informed us that he had sent a parcel to our Johannesburg Head Office containing four products that were poisoned with cyanide and, unless he was paid a given ransom, four similar products would be introduced randomly into Gauteng stores. When that first call came through, we were already well versed, through years and years of training, in crisis management techniques.

After 1982, when US company Johnson & Johnson created a template for managing incidents of malicious tampering with products, companies revisited their capacities globally for coping with such crises. In the Johnson & Johnson scenario, a disaffected person tampered with Tylenol – a headache remedy – which resulted in several deaths in the USA.

At the first indication of a problem with Tylenol (at the time the holder of a 35 per cent market share), the parent company Johnson & Johnson immediately recalled every unit of the product from outlets across the world and swung into action to develop new, tamper-proof packaging.

The tampering episode reduced the product's market share to almost zero in the immediate aftermath of reports of casualties, but the parent company's clear demonstration that they placed the safety and wellbeing of consumers above market share resulted in a rapid recovery for Tylenol sales. Johnson & Johnson, furthermore, won widespread approval for the moral stand they had taken in dealing with the crisis.

Everyone learned from this copybook example of sound and ethical crisis management. As part of the process of establishing our own Risk Analysis Profile, Pick 'n Pay had already started consulting with specialists at the time of the Tylenol incident, consultation that included ongoing methods of countering mischievous tampering.

When, in 2003 Pick 'n Pay received a call from an anonymous male saying that a parcel he had sent to our Johannesburg Head Office contained four products laced with cyanide and four similar products would be introduced randomly into our Gauteng stores, we were well versed in crisis management techniques.

The 2003 extortionist incident: a case study

Immediately following that first call from the extortionist in 2003, the four products he had mailed to us were taken to a laboratory for testing. Very soon thereafter we received dreadful news: the laboratory reported that – just as the extortionist claimed – the products contained traces of cyanide. After profound consultations with the specialist consultants we had already called in to advise us and to help with the police investigation, we decided not to go public since there were no poisoned goods in our stores at that stage. Both our expert consultants and the South African Police concurred with our decision, pointing out that going public at that stage, when consumers were not in any danger, might well cause the extortionist to go to ground, breaking our channels of communication with him and his dangerous agenda.

Meanwhile, a war of nerves was being waged between Pick 'n Pay and the extortionist, whose methods of communication came straight off the pages of some second-rate thriller. Coded classified advertisements, to which we had to reply in prearranged code, conveyed instructions for setting up meetings at which the ransom could change hands. Getting to pay the extortionist's demand proved frustrating. Our agent would be sent from venue to venue, following a paper trail of instructions in true spy-thriller style but, as the cat-and-mouse game continued, the ransom money was never collected.

The second round of the saga opened when, one chilling day, the extortionist made it known that he had randomly placed four specific items into Gauteng stores, each clearly marked, 'Poison. Do not eat.'

An immediate and thorough search of all hypermarkets, supermarkets and family-franchised stores was initiated and three marked items were found. At the very time that arrangements were being made to withdraw all units of the four products, regardless of whether or not they showed signs of tampering, and a public statement was being prepared, a woman telephoned to say that she had become very ill after having eaten some tinned fish, which she later noticed was marked 'Poison'.

Once this became public, the floodgates opened and we were suddenly inundated with calls. People claimed that they, their children, even their cats and dogs, had become ill after eating products purchased from a Pick 'n Pay store.

In response, we decided that *any* product named as suspect would be pulled from stores without further question and, of course, any medical expenses incurred would be recompensed whether the incident was a proven case of poisoning or some routine gastric ailment incorrectly identified as poison-related. At the time,

I was out of the country on sabbatical leave and had to be restrained almost physically from jumping on a plane to fly home. I lived on the telephone in constant contact with the crisis 'nerve centre' in South Africa.

An important point to mention at this stage, and to bear in mind for future developments, is this: every time a product was sent to local laboratories for analysis, reports came back positive. One such report even stated that a batch of products contained 'enough poison to kill 10 cows'.

These were deeply troubling times. There had been occasions in the history of Pick 'n Pay when the company came under severe attack, particularly during periods of labour unrest and industrial action, but no onslaught had ever seemed quite so malicious and mischievous as the 2003 extortion crisis.

When, however, the crisis reached its highest point of awfulness, as though in compensation, a huge amount of warmth and support came our grateful way.

President Thabo Mbeki, Mr Mandela and a long list of celebrated citizens called to express their solidarity. Best of all were the 10 000 calls received over one two-day period from ordinary members of the public – some Pick 'n Pay customers, some not – who stated that an attack on Pick 'n Pay was an attack on all South Africans. In their thousands, people expressed their appreciation for the honest and direct way that Sean Summers and his team were handling the crisis and said, overwhelmingly, that the poison scare had encouraged rather than discouraged them from shopping at Pick 'n Pay. So many people told us that they refused to be cowed; they wanted to show their contempt for the terror tactics of the extortionist.

The extent and quality of the public outpouring of support during the 2003 crisis turned out to be the warmest affirmation that there was an entrenched belief that Pick 'n Pay placed the safety of people shopping at our stores above any other consideration. The support, concern and professionalism of the South African Police during the crisis is something we also gratefully acknowledge and deeply appreciate.

So it is that when counting the costs of the 2003 crisis – very extensive costs, which included massive consultancy fees and media charges, medical costs and an estimated R15-million loss of profit and sales on withdrawn products – one overwhelming conclusion remained: at the end of the day, the warmth, understanding and support we received made up a thousand times for each cent outlaid.

At the height of the crisis, absolutely out of the blue, there came a twist so bizarre that everyone was left gasping in amazement.

For added verification, the same samples that had been tested in local laboratories were sent overseas for similar testing. Imagine our astonishment when reports came back from *both* sources outside South Africa confirming that no product had tested positive for traces of cyanide any higher than those expected to be found naturally. The news came as a bombshell. It was not the poison but the small holes drilled into packaging (the holes through which the poison was purported to have been introduced) that had caused the cases of illness that had been reported.

A strange turn of events indeed.

The extortionist has not, at the time of writing, been apprehended, but the crisis he occasioned has taught us, as individuals and as a company, important lessons. One of those lessons, certainly, is that we need to learn more about the food we sell, and for this we must look to our scientists and food technicians. I, for one, had absolutely no idea that cyanide is a naturally occurring substance in the human body.

The conduct of Pick 'n Pay's people during the crisis was exemplary. Sean Summers, Jonathan Ackerman, David Robins and Nick Badminton, Pick 'n Pay's crisis leaders, reassured the public with their honesty and managed the essential practicalities with decisive strength. The secretaries who stayed at their desks until midnight to field calls from the public, receptionists who handled callers calmly, with tact and courtesy, and the wonderful team of Customer Service Managers who fielded the majority of the thousands of calls that flooded in were all remarkable.

Then, of course, there was the wonderful public reaction that could not have been more flattering or more deeply appreciated. Throughout this crisis, the South African public again demonstrated its refusal to be intimidated, threatened or bullied.

In a December 2003 public poll, Pick 'n Pay was pronounced the most trustworthy company in the country. International experience shows that companies caught up in extortion crises invariably experience a decline in public trust, even though the public perceives that the crisis was not of the company's own making. In our case, not only did our share prices remain impervious to events, it even transpired that most customers around South Africa, rather than staying away out of fear, were making a point of shopping at Pick 'n Pay to express their solidarity with us. Inevitably, however, the extortion crisis did cause the loss of a large amount of turnover.

Media relations

In the main, I believe that celebrities and businesses have the relationship with the press that they deserve. South Africa has one of the freest presses in the world and we, as a company, have enormous respect for the high ethical code most of the media subscribe to.

As a point of policy, we never knowingly mislead the media, and make sure that when we do have something to say, it is an informed point of view. In order to do this, all spokespeople do their part by reading major national and regional newspapers as early as possible each morning, and monitoring radio and television bulletins, so that queries can be coherently answered.

Where issues of direct relevance to Pick 'n Pay crop up – debate around food prices, for instance – we communicate among ourselves even earlier so that anything that needs to be done within the company is put in hand and, most importantly, we speak with one voice. A coherent, readily available response has been one of the secrets of our success in building strong and mutually respectful relations with the media.

Under the Third Leg of the Table, our policy of decentralisation in our relationships with the media creates a degree of individual freedom among Pick 'n Pay people that is rare anywhere in the corporate world. Regional managers and even individual store managers are mandated to comment on issues of pricing, on our company in general and on people-related issues as they apply to that particular person or place. Where major issues – say, in respect of a rumoured takeover – are concerned, comment comes only from the offices of the Chairman, CEO or the Financial Director.

Although it is generally unusual for regional managers to be given the opportunity to build their own relationships with local media, we believe that the overwhelmingly favourable publicity Pick 'n Pay receives regionally as a result of this freedom can only be favourable for the company.

Furthermore, regional or store managers who are encouraged to make their own comments in fact run their own media-relations policy and consequently feel more in control of their own destiny. Since national issues relating to commodity prices or policies are discussed between ourselves early on the mornings of breaking news, a national standpoint is established for communication to the media at large without compromising local responses.

Although as a company we always endeavour to sing from the same song sheet, individual media interpretations may differ. However, we do make allowances for a margin of error, and when these errors do occur they are certainly not enough of an issue to force us to rethink our existing policy of decentralised media relations.

Social responsibility

Profits are the bloodstream of the economic world, but social responsibility should be woven right through a business person's whole existence.

Writing about the role of social responsibility in business, Milton Friedman – Nobel prize-winning elder statesman and icon of twentieth-century economic thinking – once maintained that executives who over-expended on issues of social responsibility, in terms of funding, time and commitment, were nothing more than cheats. They were thieves of shareholders' money. The basis for Friedman's deeply shocking – at least to my mind – opinion, rested on the theory that the sole job of business executives was to maximise profits for shareholders (the approach termed 'shareholder value'), while it was the job of governments to look after issues of social responsibility, funded from company taxation.

The 'shareholder' value – the 'me' philosophy that maintained that companies existed solely to promote the interests of their shareholders – suffered the severest of reversals in the aftermath of big-name corporate collapses that continue to punctuate global commerce. Among these was the implosion of US blue-chip company Enron (then the world's seventh-largest company), amid a welter of malpractice and corporate immorality. The Enron collapse brought afresh into international focus issues surrounding good corporate governance.

At the time Enron began to unravel, the company was renowned for its philanthropic support for scores of charities and causes. It had been corporate practice to donate 1 per cent of its earnings to charitable organisations. Even the company's harshest critics admit that this did a great deal of good.

Gottlieb Duttweiler, the philanthropic tycoon who founded the Swiss Migros empire, expounded, lived and traded according to the theory that the more a business gives, the more it gets back – in other words, the theory of 'enlightened self-interest'. However, generous corporate giving is not enlightened if accounting acrobatics are, at the same time, deliberately falsifying the books; giving to charities that support people who have fallen on hard times is not enlightened if internal pension funds, for instance, are being impoverished at the same time.

There is no human need, no category of education and training, no medical condition or handicap relating to any age group, either gender or any major religious belief that has not at some time or another, many on an ongoing basis, received support in terms of Pick 'n Pay's broad-based programmes of social responsibility.

Social responsibility ranks among the most revered of the core values on which Pick 'n Pay has been built, and on which the company is sustained. Various budgets have been tailored over the years to meet the vast number of social responsibility initiatives with which Pick 'n Pay is involved. We have, for instance, a Chairman's Budget (which I administer), a CEO's Budget (administered by Sean Summers), and a General Manager's Budget (which Nic Badminton administers). In addition, each regional General Manager has his or her own budget, as have each manager and each store.

A separate budget for donations in excess of R250 000 exists in order to ensure that projects of this scope are generally aired before being approved, both so as to be certain that money has not already been given from another budget elsewhere in the company and to gain the approval of the Executive Committee for the donation itself.

As a general policy – although we prefer to be flexible and open to suggestion – we do not allocate very large sums to sports sponsorships, because this would detract from giving to smaller, more immediate, grass-roots beneficiaries. Although millions are donated on a regular basis, we believe quite firmly that the ordinary person raising funds for his church bazaar, the woman caring for six AIDS orphans in a township and the scheme offering a daily cup of soup and a slice of bread to hungry schoolchildren are as worthy of help as a hospital that needs a multimillion-rand piece of equipment.

Social initiatives and policy principles

Paramount in the administration of Pick 'n Pay's social responsibility programmes is the non-partisan nature of our responses. In my 50 years' experience running retail organisations, I have, sometimes bitterly, come to understand that it is impossible to please all the people all the time. Nevertheless, Pick 'n Pay has, for example, supported Christian, Hindu, Jewish and Muslim causes at every stage of our development.

Responding to disasters

In providing disaster relief, speed is an imperative. Keeping ample cash reserves on call – as we do under the company's First (Administration) Leg – not only ensures that all the needs of our social-responsibility initiatives are met, but that they are met expeditiously.

When Serbian leader Slobodan Milosevic ordered a programme of ethnic cleansing against Kosovor Albanians in 1998, container loads of food, blankets and other essentials were despatched through the Muslim Judicial Council in South Africa with all the speed we could muster. Television images of hordes of wretched, dispossessed Muslim refugees pouring into neighbouring countries were a vivid reminder of the photographs I had seen of Jewish refugees, among them my maternal grandfather, making their way from Russia, having being summarily expelled in the latter part of the nineteenth century.

Although the South African Muslim community had, on occasion, been vocal opponents of Pick 'n Pay, we felt a strong obligation to help the Kosovor Albanians. Members of the Judicial Council later confessed to having been astonished that an organisation with a Jewish person at its head would offer assistance to Muslims in need.

Closer to home, in April 2000, within an hour of hearing desperate appeals for assistance after southern and central areas of neighbouring Mozambique, were devastated by floods, Pick 'n Pay people began gathering supplies and arranging for their distribution in Mozambique.

Responding to calls for assistance from beyond the borders of South Africa by no means lessens our awareness of need on our own doorstep. To the hundreds of thousands of South Africans who eke out a miserable existence in informal shack settlements around the country, every winter brings catastrophic flooding and every summer raging fires. Regional budgets and accounting autonomy ensure that funds for humanitarian assistance on a regional basis are instantly available.

It is a matter of great pride to Pick 'n Pay people that they are often the first to offer when such help is needed. In this way, too, public perceptions of Pick 'n Pay as part of local communities are reinforced, which returns us full circle to the theory of enlightened self-interest.

Taking the concept 'doing good is good business' and building it into every fibre of the many-faceted enterprise that Pick 'n Pay has become has been a key task in building of the company. The concept lives because the company lives by it, it is the essence of what makes us what we are.

Caring for the environment

Caring for the environment is an important extension of Pick 'n Pay's social responsibility programme. It is a broad-based policy that encompasses not only the ecology, but also social, economic, historical and cultural elements, and contains both external and internal facets.

Pick 'n Pay seeks to play a significant role in creating environmental awareness both within the company and in the minds of the general public. Consequently, each region involves itself in national environmental initiatives through the Environmental Committees in individual stores in order to take a stand in matters relating not only to the store itself but to its local community.

Internal environmental controls and programmes aim to create more value with less impact – the ideal of 'eco-efficiency'. This eco-efficiency enables more efficient production processes and the creation of better products and services, while reducing resource use, waste and pollution along the entire value chain. These eco-efficiency principles have prompted Pick 'n Pay to initiate valuable strategies relating to transport, refrigeration, energy and lighting, packaging and product technology.

The Enviro Facts Project, sponsored by Pick 'n Pay through the Worldwide Fund for Nature (WWF-SA), publishes fact sheets developed with the support of several NGOs, government departments and academic institutions. Included is serious, but accessible information accompanied by 'what you can do' features, reading lists and useful addresses.

Topical issues that tend to polarise public opinion – the genetic modification of food, food irradiation, additives – need to be handled under the same banner: find out what consumers want, and give it to them. The hotter the issue, however, the more difficult it becomes to accommodate all interests, a point well illustrated by events around the vexed question of plastic bags versus environmental issues, a controversy played out in South Africa in 2003.

The vexed issue of plastic packaging

At one point in the South African food industry, paper bags were used to package consumers' purchases but, as volumes increased and sources decreased, this option became too expensive. At that time, retailers switched to plastic bags, which were given away free with purchases and counted as a cost against expenses.

However, the irresponsible disposal of plastic bags created an untenable environmental dilemma. Tatters of plastic festooned fences across the country, piled up along roadsides, formed unsightly mountains of refuse, killed animals on land and fish in the oceans. And, since people buy food in greater quantities than any other commodity, it was the irresponsibly discarded plastic bags of major food retailers that littered the countryside in such profusion they were sardonically named South Africa's new national flower.

At a meeting in 2000 between major retailers and the government, spearheaded by then Minister of Environmental Affairs and Tourism Mr Valli Moosa, retailers were asked to agree on a cost-price figure at which plastic bags could be sold to the public (on the premise that something purchased would have a worth and would therefore not be discarded so carelessly). Government did not intend passing legislation in this regard, relying instead on a gentleman's agreement between retailers.

From the outset, that request came as a nasty shock – agreeing on a price? The word 'collusion' kept blurring our vision. Since when had Pick 'n Pay ever *agreed* on a price with competitors?

Government, however, was ignited with enthusiasm for the project and worked hard to convince food retailers that an agreed price for plastic bags could not be called price-fixing and the situation would not become competitive as long as all parties upheld their end of the bargain.

When major food retailers finally, but reluctantly, came to an agreement and fixed a price at which plastic bags would be sold, it soon became clear that other retailers had no such intention. Clothing retailers, hardware stores, small traders of every description refused to charge for their plastic bags, which naturally enough irritated the public. It seemed to them that charging for plastic had become a selective process and when they bought food, they were the victims.

At this stage, Pick 'n Pay approached the government, asking them earnestly to legislate. If charging for plastic was good for one retail industry, why not for all? Our request caused consternation.

Government, we were told, was already in trouble over the drastic reduction in the numbers of plastic bags being purchased by the retail food industry. Manufacturers of plastic reported a dire drop in demand – some citing an almost 90 per cent decrease in sales. While this was certainly good for the environment, trade unions were becoming restive over job losses, threatening militant action if their members were not protected.

Meanwhile, criticism from the public of retailers like ourselves was increasing day by day. They accused us of colluding over the price at which plastic bags were being sold – and their accusation was entirely correct. In no time at all, some retailers resolved not to charge for plastic bags at all, which prompted those that were complying to take an independent stand on what would be charged.

With confusion among retailers and consumers reigning supreme, Pick 'n Pay CEO Sean Summers visited an old and treasured friend of ours, Irish chain-store owner Feargal Quinn, to see first-hand the environmentally friendly green bags Feargal's Irish stores sold to shoppers. Sean immediately recognised that these sturdy, long-lasting, lightweight bags would be as perfect in

South Africa as they were in Ireland. With the consent of Feargal, it was decided that Pick 'n Pay would buy in quantities of Green Bags, to be sold in South Africa at cost, with a small donation from each sale going to environmental charity.

Those first Green Bags, which went on sale in South Africa for R5 each, flew out of the stores so speedily it took our breath away. We immediately made arrangements to have our own version of the bags manufactured in South Africa, which would help revive local bag manufacturers stricken by the ban on plastic. And, since 5.5 million Green Bags had been sold by early 2004, they also became a marvellous marketing tool.

On the introduction of Green Bags, we also set our own prices for the sale of plastic bags to those customers who wanted to buy them and instantly began lowering prices of products on our shelves from the proceeds of money collected on the sale of packaging.

We are completely happy with what we are doing by charging our own reduced price for the sale of bags, making a really affordable and workable alternative available, encouraging conservation by making donations to environmental causes and reducing the price of foodstuffs with funds from packaging charges, while continuing to support all our well-organised, long-standing environmental initiatives and those of the government. Naturally enough, a great cry of 'foul' went up from competitors when Pick 'n Pay decided to disentangle from the inconsistencies that had gathered around what was essentially an admirable, but mismanaged, attempt to make South Africa cleaner.

Investing in education and literacy

Pick 'n Pay's programme of social investment is perhaps at its most important when concentrated on ways of ensuring secure futures through education, based on the recognition of every individual's unique potential. The company has elected to help realise that potential in as many of South Africa's people as possible.

The Pick 'n Pay Foundation has promoted literacy across South Africa through its support for the Booksmart Foundation, which has facilitated the collection of books from schools and universities in the USA for distribution among needy schools and ill-equipped universities locally.

To help foster local education, Pick 'n Pay's subsidiary Score Supermarkets provide accessible basic adult education in literacy and numeracy through the provision of free learning materials for customers. In an innovative and practical application, this learning is further facilitated by the in-store radio station before normal trading hours for interaction with staff.

By the year 2004, the Ackerman Family Educational Trust had assisted more than 200 students to graduate over a period of 10 years. Of these, 35 have graduated as medical doctors.

Post 1994, the company's policy-makers in the field of bursary funding came to the conclusion that intervention was desperately needed in order to equip previously disadvantaged matriculants to cope with the rigours of competitive tertiary education. Many of these young people, who had already achieved a great triumph in obtaining their school-leaving matriculation after years spent struggling through school systems that could often not even provide running water or a building let alone suitably qualified people to teach them, were finally overwhelmed by the pace of higher-learning institutions, long established to cater to the needs and talents of privileged students.

Accordingly, under the auspices of the Pick 'n Pay Chairman's Budget, a bridging scheme was initiated through the University of Cape Town, with the stated intention of levelling the playing fields. This initiative and various important offshoots have proved paramount in developing opportunities for underprivileged learners.

Funding the arts

Many prominent figures concerned with the funding of the arts have noted that the present South African government's efforts at levelling the playing field – by providing a measure of national funding for all the arts in a democratic manner – have resulted in an overall shortfall of arts funding. Compared to what is required, critically little is received by all.

Without contributions from the private sector, therefore, the development of artistic skills is under siege. Insufficient funding equals an insufficient number of artists, the smallest number of whom come from disadvantaged communities who tend, naturally, to be more concerned about buying food than sending their children to dance classes.

The cast of world-class performers who have emerged out of Pick 'n Pay bursary funding testifies to the fact that South Africa has no shortage of talent, merely a shortage of cash through which it might be nurtured.

Abel Moeng, born in Thabane, a dusty, deprived township just outside Rustenburg, in the province of Limpopo, is an example of the success of bursary funding, which has taken this otherwise resourceless young singer to stages in South Africa, the USA and Europe, where he has delighted some of the world's most discriminating opera audiences.

Acclaimed opera star Dr Sidwell Hartman, a member of Cape Town's previously disadvantaged coloured community, is another. Through bursary funding, Pick 'n Pay assisted him in studying at the renowned Juilliard School in New York, which in turn led to a glittering career that included singing, to great critical acclaim, at London's Covent Garden opera house. With a doctorate conferred on him by the University of Cape Town, Sidwell teaches new generations of artists at the university's School of Music while continuing to honour international performance commitments.

Mamela Nyamza proceeded, via tuition at the Pick 'n Pay-funded Zama dance school in the township of Gugulethu outside Cape Town, to dance with the New York Ballet. In 2004, Mamelia triumphed over hundreds of hopeful dancers, who trained with the best companies in the world, to win a starring role in *The Lion King*, staged in London.

Since performing with the Cape Town Philharmonic Orchestra as a child protégée, the young violinist Zoë Beyers has continued to dazzle the most discerning international audiences. Teachers accustomed to working with pupils from the cream of European music schools have been extremely impressed by Zoë, a proudly South African performer, whose advancing academic and musical career we, as a company, are proud to sponsor.

Funding sports

Although, at first sight, it might seem unconventional to link social responsibility to sport, this is in fact a natural, sensible and mutually empowering link. By applying creative ideas to sports sponsorship, it is possible to ensure handsome payouts to charity whether the sponsored team wins or loses.

Thus, when South Africa's Springboks left to compete in the 2003 Rugby World Cup in Australia, they left with a pledge from Pick 'n Pay that R1 500 would be paid to charity for every Springbok try scored. Even though the Springboks finished a disappointing fifth in the world rankings and were knocked out of the competition in the quarterfinals, a cheque for R150 000 was handed over to a needy charity.

Meanwhile, a unique opportunity for South Africa to lead the world in sports development in schools has been identified by Professor Tim Noakes, world-renowned sports scientist, whose Cape Town-based Sports Science Institute has received Pick 'n Pay funding. As Professor Noakes has remarked: 'Regardless of the pre-eminent advantages to their health, the lessons children learn from participating in sport have overwhelming benefits for the process of nation-building.'

The people of South Africa, as a whole, have gained a massive boost by winning the right to host the 2010 Soccer World Cup. Although this might not be immediately apparent, hosting the Soccer World Cup is likely to be the greatest and most ambitious project for social responsibility that South Africa has envisaged since Cape Town's abortive bid to host the 2004 summer Olympics.

Quite apart from the obvious advantages likely to flow from hosting the 2010 Soccer World Cup – thousands of jobs, business opportunities benefiting formal and informal trade and industry –

the organisers of the event and the government of South Africa will be tasked with tackling a whole gamut of social ills and problems of infrastructure before hundreds of thousands of guests arrive to put South Africa under the glaring spotlight of international scrutiny.

Residents of visible informal settlements, transport and travel networks and infrastructure, the building industry, accommodation providers and purveyors of every saleable commodity imaginable are all in line to benefit from what will have to be a drive to polish up South Africa's real image. The opposite fate is reserved for crime and criminals, death-trap conveyances and other scars on the face of South Africa.

Clearly, all who deserve to win stand to win.

Third Leg points to remember

- Sound cash management under the First Leg of the Table ensures adequate funding for programmes of social responsibility under the Third Leg.
- Everything done under the Third Leg is done to please customers and to contribute towards fulfilling Pick 'n Pay's role in society.
- In addition to making major donations, it is important to be in a position to help with as many small requests as possible.
- Public relations are lived, not bought.
- Time is worth more than money when it comes to cementing good public relations.
- The Pick 'n Pay 'brand' has arisen indirectly around the main aim of pursuing the interests of consumer sovereignty.
- In general, celebrities and businesses have the relationship they deserve with the media. In this context, it is important to be available to the media and to speak with one informed, honest voice.
- First Leg cash reserves are essential in providing speedy disaster relief.
- Care for the environment is a key extension of social responsibility.
- Social investment is based on the premise of the individual's unique potential.

9

The Fourth Leg: People

❝ You can dream, create, design and build the most wonderful place in the world, but it requires people to make the dream a reality. ❞

(Walt Disney)

IN THE VOLATILE field of personnel relations, Pick 'n Pay has inevitably seen good times and bad, ups and downs. Throughout, however, we have made it a priority to provide our people with the best workplace experience. This is a prime reason why we want to have healthy cash reserves (an administrative, First Leg function), a fundamental policy that has enabled us to fund a range of benefits recognised as among the most comprehensive offered in South Africa.

Allied to the issue of welfare is that of opportunity, including the provision of educational bursaries and formal workplace training. Such considerations caused the various phases of Vuselela – the most significant programmes the company has ever implemented. Vuselela redefined the Fourth Leg of our table and, in so doing, redirected all our fortunes.

Experiences that frustrated my own career, up until the time I acquired Pick 'n Pay, have had an enormous influence on the way I have chosen to fulfil my role within the company. The development of Pick 'n Pay's policy of decentralisation, for instance, arose directly as a reaction to a past career in which I had experienced first-hand the frustrations of feeling like an insignificant cog in a wheel, even though the cog I had been was of considerable importance in driving the wheel that restricted me.

As Pick 'n Pay evolved, all our efforts have become focused on making people feel important as individuals, which has proved to be a great way to build a business. We take particular pride, meanwhile, in standing behind our people in times of trouble. This type of compassion is a vital component of the fundamental core values of care and respect that are built into the working model of the Four Legs of the Table.

The discussion that follows covers many of the issues that arise under the Fourth Leg of Pick 'n Pay's table – the leg that can be said to contain the 'corporate soul' of the company for it is here that we concentrate on supporting and developing our 'brand's' best asset: the people of Pick 'n Pay.

This discussion concludes with an important issue that falls within the parameters of the Fourth Leg, namely succession planning in a family-owned business. Putting in place a fair, equitable, practical and workable plan for the time when I step down from the chairmanship is crucial to the future of this family-owned business. It is an endeavour into which I have poured, and continue to pour, massive amounts of time, thought and energy.

The soul of a corporation

Well before an incredulous international audience witnessed its unexpected collapse, Enron – once the world's seventh largest company – had earned a less-than-enviable reputation among at least one group of individuals: the people it employed.

The black drama of Enron's final demise was, in fact, merely the final curtain brought down on a production that had been played out against the backdrop of a corporate culture so base it not only deliberately and routinely fired one fifth of its workforce annually, but based those dismissals on assessments carried out among colleagues. The climate of distrust and insecurity those denouncements must have engendered can well be imagined. People were encouraged to plot against one another, to dissemble rather than cooperate in promoting the wellbeing of the company's business.

Building a corporate climate in which people are proud to work for a company, not just for its performance on the stock exchange or for the profits it makes, but for the way it cares for its own, is one of the best tools for promoting productivity. In nurturing the needs of loyal employees, and consequently those of their families too, it is the charity that starts at home that builds the company and boosts the bottom line.

In our early trading days, when Pick 'n Pay comprised just a few stores concentrated in the Western Cape region, my wife and I started what has become the tradition of visiting stores at Christmas time to make personal contact with as many of our people as possible, to hear how they, and the stores in which they worked, have fared. Today, year-end visits are shared among top management. Given, however, that by 2004 there were 351 corporate outlets (excluding the Australian chain, franchise stores, TM Supermarkets and Auto Centres), these annual pilgrimages remain epic. We cannot physically see everyone, but we are all aware that each hand shaken belongs to an individual and that every individual's contribution is respected.

In my own case, long experience in year-end calls has given me a finely tuned antenna that picks up undertones bubbling beneath the surface. When I visit a store and detect disharmonious vibrations, it will not be long before someone comes to tell me that they have a sick child, or that they are ill with worry over financial problems. Sometimes the store manager will tell me that he *knows* something is wrong, but cannot identify what it is.

At the start of every new working year, therefore, all the 'visitors' return with foolscap pages full of notes and 'things to do' and the information is disseminated among the people who are in a position to remedy each particular problem. Regardless of who is delegated to help, no issue raised on the annual visit circuit is allowed simply to be forgotten.

Large returns in loyalty come from small gestures, such as sending a personal note to someone who has been promoted or making sure that the family of a person who has been transferred is happily settled – we work hard to avoid the mistake of thinking that people can be moved around like chess pieces on a board. Such gestures should be made anyway in the name of simple courtesy.

When I say that independent polls repeatedly name Pick 'n Pay as one of the most admired companies in South Africa, I am not trying to give ourselves a pat on the back. What I do want to express is my belief that our place on 'Top Ten' approval-rated company lists happens from time to time because – despite the odd thoughtless lapse – we adhere unswervingly to the core values and ethics built into each of the Four Legs of our table.

Prioritising ethics over all else, particularly in terms of the Fourth – People – Leg, is one of the soundest and best-proven pieces of advice I can share.

Promotion from within

Throughout my career prior to buying my own company, I had witnessed, like most employees, occasions of disappointment, despondency and even despair when the hiring of an outsider to fill some post within an organisation dashed the hopes and aspirations of those within the 'family'.

When I was at last able to control matters of employment within my own business, I resolved from the beginning that loyalty and dedication would not only be rewarded monetarily but with promotion, as and when new opportunities occurred or someone retired or resigned. Promoting from within has thus, over the years, become a core value of Pick 'n Pay's employment charter.

Our current CEO, Sean Summers, is visible evidence of how seriously we take this policy within the company.

Sean's late father once asked me if I could find a place in Pick 'n Pay for his restless son, who did not know what to do with himself. Sean started work with Pick 'n Pay at a humble level, but every time I came across him, packing out fruit and vegetables, supervising a back door, organising displays, he would put his case for moving up the ladder, urgently and insistently.

'Make me a manager, make me a junior buyer, make me a senior buyer' went the refrain, sung to the tune of the formidable energy and industrious talent he always displayed.

In April 1999, Sean reached the pinnacle of promotion when we announced his appointment as Pick 'n Pay's CEO, a reward he richly deserved, not least for his remarkable efforts at turning the company around following a time of great turmoil after 1994.

In general, I always say that interview day is a prospective employee's best day. At an interview, only the good is on view and the warts remain firmly under wraps. Employees of some standing, however, you know – warts and all. You know the best and you know the worst, which makes a sound case for the cause, and the sense, of promoting from within.

Reaching for the stars

One of the situations that I recall most vividly from the time I worked as a store section manager for the Greatermans Group in Johannesburg happened when I received notification that a delegation of top management was scheduled to visit the store on the following day.

I remember setting to work with a will to spruce up my section, supervising cleaning and polishing, wiping down all the shelves and repacking them in pristine order, working on my own until late that night in readiness for The Visit.

The next day, as I hovered around my section, the visitors suddenly appeared at the end of an aisle in my section, all clad clone-like in identical tailored greatcoats and homburg hats. They filed silently past the immaculate shelves and fresh floor displays that I had worked until midnight to prepare. They moved silently through like a host of expressionless wraiths, looking neither left nor right, and did not even acknowledge my presence, let alone offer a greeting or comment. In less than a minute they had gone, leaving me feeling foolish and slighted.

Out of that humiliating experience – being treated so shabbily that I felt of no worth or consequence to the organisation that employed me – has grown a system of identifying what we call 'stars' within Pick 'n Pay. On visits to stores, both small and large, I make a special point of identifying people, people with potential, who are putting extra effort into whichever area of employment they occupy. People so identified are marked by store, regional and national management as 'stars', to be specially nurtured in terms of being given training opportunities and performance bonuses.

In my experience, a bowl of flowers sent with a personal note of congratulation to a lady who has been recognised for excellence and promoted from a lowly position pays handsome dividends in loyalty and commitment. Being punctilious about sending letters of congratulation to staff who have been promoted or, for that matter, letters of commiseration to the bereaved, are small matters of courtesy that everyone appreciates – and remembers.

Decentralisation

By the time I bought the small Pick 'n Pay chain in 1967, I had already assimilated the theory of the Four Legs of the Table and the concept of the supremacy of the consumer in retailing. However, it was not until I became the owner of my own enterprise that I had the opportunity to properly implement those – quite revolutionary at the time – ideas.

I opened the doors of Pick 'n Pay equipped with the basic structure around which I knew I would build the business. Also, like the proverbial new broom, I intended sweeping away all vestiges of policy and practice that had so frustrated me as an, albeit senior, employee. Back in 1967, I was young, energetic and utterly captivated by the freedom to run my own small business as I saw fit.

One of the worst aspects of working for the big organisation I had come from was feeling powerless to make independent decisions on matters that impacted upon one's own field of endeavour. Thus, although I had been a competent General Manager with a performance to prove it, I had had no say over the prices set for goods sold in the stores I controlled.

I had tried very hard to implement ideas relating to organisation, social responsibility and marketing that I had eagerly assimilated on learning visits to the USA, but I was mostly frustrated in those efforts, firstly because it was just so difficult to penetrate the inner sanctums, the offices of the policy-makers, to discuss anything at all, and secondly because independent action was frowned upon. After numerous abortive efforts to secure a hearing, I would think quietly to myself that a day had to come when I could shape policies according to my own discretion and inclination.

One of the key policies around which Pick 'n Pay is organised – our policy of decentralisation and the allied flat organisational chart to which we adhere – grew from those very frustrations. As our policy has evolved, the Pick 'n Pay Group has been restructured accordingly, so that at national level only three Managing Directors and one General Manager report to today's CEO, Sean Summers.

Regional autonomy

It is at regional level that our policy of decentralisation impacts most surely on the dynamism that has become a benchmark of the company. By applying the principle of working with an organisational chart that is as flat as possible, regional general managers report directly to just one line below the Chairman. Regional managers are well aware that controls are in place, but generally thrive in an atmosphere where they are held by a lighter-than-usual rein.

Each of the five supermarket regions – Western Cape, Eastern Cape, KwaZulu-Natal, Gauteng and the Northern Region – drives its own marketing, based on its own idiosyncrasies. Since each region has its own operational, marketing and social responsibility budget, there is a high degree of local regional 'flavour'. Each region may choose to support charities or projects that impact directly on the day-to-day lives of customers.

In each region, there are weekly management meetings to discuss administrative problems, marketing and advertising problems, people and social responsibility in relation to that localised entity. Regions are also spurred by intense competitiveness – each store wants to have the best record for social responsibility projects, for caring for the environment and so on in order to boost the overall performance of the region.

At regional level, each store is responsible for its own bottom-line results, and these depend entirely on the nature of customers shopping at that particular branch. Customers' needs, pricing policies, even social responsibility programmes vary from branch to branch and from region to region, each of which has its own warehouse, its own buyers, employs its own people and strikes its own balance sheet.

The policy of decentralisation within Pick 'n Pay has succeeded because it makes each region focus on its own collective strengths and abilities, building team spirit to serve customers better. Individual store managers and their staff really do become part of the communities they serve and the environment in which they operate. As a Fourth Leg principle, decentralisation is indeed a magnificent empowerment tool. People do not see themselves as insignificant cogs in a mighty wheel that turns relentlessly without respect for autonomy or independence.

I would even go so far as to say that decentralisation holds the key to all our future expansion. As a general principle, the flatter a company can make its organisational chart, the better it is for the company.

Investing in people

In 1994, Pick 'n Pay was hit by one of the most vicious strikes in South Africa's history. As I looked out of the window of my office in Cape Town at yet another scene of riot and mayhem, it suddenly occurred to me that the strike crisis our company was facing could signal the end of everything I had worked so incredibly hard to achieve.

By far the worst result of the 1994 strike was that the warm and mutually sustaining relationship that had existed between workers and management now lay in tatters. A sullen air pervaded our workplaces and we all suffered, wondering how to go forward.

It was at this point, when morale had reached rock bottom, that CEO Sean Summers and Martin Rosen, then the Marketing Director, conceived the first phase of a brilliant plan they named Vuselela, an Nguni word meaning 'rebirth'.

If Pick 'n Pay, post 1994, was to not only get up and get on but to reclaim the values and rediscover the core on which the company was built, heroic measures had to be taken. What was needed was a massive investment that would aim at restoring morale and rekindling pride in our people so that they, in turn, could go back to greeting our customers with smiles rather than curses.

The 1994 strike

The most painful aspect of those dark days in 1994 was that, as a company trading in the new South Africa, we least deserved to be so targeted. There was, and is, no question that Pick 'n Pay has had a long and constant record for championing the rights of our own people, and for vigorously promoting non-racialism and promotion on merit long before South Africa democratised.

The timing of the 1994 strike could not have been worse or more unexpected. Divided, fragmented, tortured, South Africa had managed somehow, despite formidable odds accompanied by devastating levels of violence, the astonishing feat of holding a first all-race election in April of that year – an election achieved not through bloody revolution as almost all had predicted, but through a process of negotiation.

Everything that people of goodwill from all races had dreamed of and hoped for had happened right here in South Africa in April 1994. Apartheid had been dismantled and Nelson Mandela, the nation's figurehead, icon, heart and soul, had assumed the presidency, presiding over a government of national unity.

The world welcomed South Africa back into the fold of nations with open arms; in fact, our nation became *the* universal symbol of hope by proving that words were, indeed, the mightiest sword.

In the midst of all this euphoria, however, dark plots were afoot. The African National Congress (ANC) government led by Mr Mandela governed as a tripartite alliance comprising the ANC, the Congress of South African Trades Unions (COSATU) and the South African Communist Party (SACP). Naturally enough, the two weaker parties to the alliance – COSATU and the SACP – were worried by the dominance of the mighty ANC.

Accordingly, as I was later informed by a man from a union unrelated to ours, COSATU decided to target figurehead companies for industrial action to show too-happy and too-successful Mr Mandela just how much power they wielded. When it came to choosing victims, big, high-profile Pick 'n Pay presented a perfect target, particularly as the company was, at that time, already engaged in wage negotiations that were not proceeding smoothly.

Talks between the company and union representatives became increasingly acrimonious. Attitudes among the union and its members hardened and Pick 'n Pay staff turned militant. Their parades on shop floors hampered trade and, much worse, shoppers – our sovereign consumers – began to be seriously threatened and intimidated.

The dark banks of hostility built up, layer upon layer, until a strike was finally called. During the first week or so, the ferocity displayed by some Pick 'n Pay employees participating in the strike shocked me to the core. Shoppers who did try to venture into stores were spat at, manhandled, taunted and terrorised. As I watched television news bulletins, night after dreadful night, showing baying mobs of strikers smashing windows and insulting shoppers, I felt ill at the futility and shamefulness of it all. One night, my wife and I narrowly escaped being attacked by a screaming mob of roving picketers out looking for trouble.

I began to dread answering my telephone at work, for I had started to receive horrible, blood-curdling death threats. And as the strike reached a peak of awfulness I began to fear that the slide into chaos might be irreversible. But, as all bad things will, the strike did finally end – leaving in its wake a trail of devastation and heartbreak. Our treasured and long-nurtured consumers had been forced to stay away from Pick 'n Pay stores, causing the first drop in profit ever recorded since 1967.

Scores of small traders who shared premises with us in shopping centres suffered tragically. They lost their livelihoods, becoming helpless cannon fodder caught in the crossfire. The strike also slashed net profits viciously, making it – paradoxically – increasingly difficult to fund the unreasonable wage increases the union demanded. The strikers themselves suffered serious setbacks, having gone without wages for four weeks. Suddenly, people who had been gainfully employed, with access to benefits unparalleled in the local retail industry, could not feed their families: union funds did not put bread on bare tables or pay school fees.

Vuselela in the context of the new South Africa

As CEO Sean Summers put it, *The underpinning principle is that we can only grow our company through growing people.*

Post 1994, management had to furnish the funds to launch Vuselela, the campaign of 'rebirth' we had decided to embark upon, and accept that well meant as our previous management style had been, it had perhaps been too paternalistic and therefore out of step with what was expected of employers in the new South Africa.

In the aftermath of the strike, certain unpalatable home truths also became known to us, such as the fact that around 40 per cent of hourly-paid Pick 'n Pay staffers were illiterate. Under the auspices of Vuselela, agreements were thus signed with institutions, including the South African Technikon, a tertiary institution that had already examined and endorsed 456 training modules created and developed by Pick 'n Pay.

These modules, covering skills across the employee spectrum, ranged from Adult Basic Education and Training (ABET) for those previously denied formal education to internationally recognised MBA degrees. Emphasis was placed on structured on-the-job training. Employees were to be able to learn at their own pace in real-life situations with management taking co-responsibility for their development.

The Vuselela education initiative ushered in the era of graduation ceremonies that have since been held all around South Africa. At graduations, employees – suitably attired in academic gowns and mortar boards – receive matriculation certificates, Pick 'n Pay diplomas in basic literacy and other higher qualifications.

A crucial component of the campaign was to restore morale within the company and to foster pride in achievement. So it was that learning trips to the Disney Institute in Orlando, USA, were instigated as rewards and as recognition for outstanding service to the company and to our sovereign consumers. These trips to the USA allowed our people to learn from those most professional of professionals and have proved to be a great motivator, one of the many strands woven into the fabric of the Vuselela campaign.

Vuselela, brain child of Sean Summers and Martin Rosen, to whom I shall always be deeply grateful for their stroke of genius in conceiving it and for their energy and commitment in driving it, replenished the depleted stream uniting our people and brought about the rebirth of the morals and core values that have always defined Pick 'n Pay.

The campaign also ushered in an era marked by a frenzy of rebuilding, refurbishing and remodelling on such a scale it was terrifying. Following a round of trips in which the brightest and best retail stores in Europe were studied, a programme was initiated to make over each and every Pick 'n Pay store in South Africa. The ensuing mess and confusion were unbelievable – it took every ounce of faith we could muster to see our way through the piles of rubble that our business had become to the fresh new-look stores promised at the end of it all.

Eventually, though, like a phoenix rising from the ashes, every store emerged refurbished, refitted and rejuvenated. The best customer-pleasing features – most notably the 'fresh' sections of the new stores – stood ready to serve as a backdrop for a rejuvenated workforce to return to the solid values of doing everything we could, willingly, efficiently and with a smile, for our customers.

Our decision to pour billions into Vuselela to restore morale and rebuild customer confidence was contentious, coming, as it did, at a time when the R1.5 billion spent on refurbishment alone might have been used to buy ailing opposition supermarket interests then on the market. But, gobbling up the opposition for the sake of simply acquiring more stores is not our management style. Personally, I have never been interested in acquiring market share for the sole purpose of empire-building, and the investment in Vuselela brought bountiful rewards out of the ashes of the 1994 strike.

Through the morale-building facets of the Vuselela concept, we introduced new uniforms, created a competition among staff from which a Vuselela song emerged, pursued the special recognition of excellence by sending staff to the Disney Institute, and looked at each and every component of how we were treating our valued customers.

Vuselela was a huge gamble, requiring us all to hold hands and collectively plunge into the unknown together. It rewarded us with a brilliant new era in which we saw Pick 'n Pay rise to unprecedented heights.

Employee benefits

Over the five years ending February 2004, some 8 500 Pick 'n Pay people have graduated from company development programmes – in-house and more formal, externally run and recognised courses stretching from six-month to three-year periods. At present, over 8 000 employees – one out of every four – are enrolled in formal training programmes. These include the 1 500 employees who are participating in Adult Basic Education and Training.

To put into practice our commitment to development of staff, a state-of-the-art Training Institute has been opened at Fourways in Johannesburg. Targeted training that exposes executives to new ways of thinking in each area of the business is ongoing, and a range of world-class programmes assist staff at all levels of management to reach their full potential.

An ever-increasing number of people embark upon and complete MBA programmes, and a CEO programme focuses on executive development and exposing people to great companies, great ideas, great initiatives and international standards. Meanwhile, over R1 million is set aside every year for educational bursaries for employees who want to pursue their studies and are in need of assistance. This assistance is extended to their families in cases where they are unable to afford the fees required for secondary or tertiary education.

Pick 'n Pay is thus justifiably proud that it is able to offer its staff one of the most comprehensive benefit programmes offered by a South African employer. As the most important internal factor in the success of the enterprise, our people deserve no less.

In every case, benefits have been carefully considered and structured. The company-subsidised medical scheme, compulsory for certain levels of employees, is owned by members and administered by outside professionals. Meanwhile, all permanent, full-time and part-time employees of the company are required to join either the Pick 'n Pay Retirement Scheme or the SACCAWU Fund. The company pays the full retirement fund contribution in the Pick 'n Pay scheme.

Funeral benefits are payable in the event of the death of a permanent employee, or the spouse, child dependant or direct parent, as defined and registered in terms of the company's funeral policy. Each employee is paid a sum of money on the death of a registered dependant.

Resident occupational health practitioners are available to employees in each region to provide professional on-site counselling on health issues, in addition to holding briefing sessions on HIV/AIDS, drug- and alcohol-related problems and the prevention of the abuse of women and children.

Employees are offered a long-service leave benefit structured according to the employee's job category. Women at Pick 'n Pay are granted nine months' maternity leave, paid at different percentages of the employee's salary. Maternity leave may also be spread over the first four years of the newborn's life, with the mother guaranteed her job or a similar job on her return. Fathers are entitled to eight fully paid days of paternity leave, from the date of the confinement, in order to bond with their newborn and support their partners.

Having a long history of involvement in peculiarly South African issues relating to housing, Pick 'n Pay seeks to alleviate the inadequate housing experienced by some staff. Company loans totalling approximately R90 million are currently in place to employees at preferential rates. Over the last decade, over R500 million has been advanced to employees to facilitate housing needs.

The acquisition of shares in the company has been described under the First Leg (Administration). Under the Pick 'n Pay Share Incentive Scheme, shares are allocated to employees on their appointment to certain levels in the company or to reward certain other achievements. Additional allocations are made as employees complete 5, 10, 15, 25 and 30 years' service. To date, more than 30 000 Pick 'n Pay employees own shares or share options in the company – acquired mainly through the Group Structure Scheme. In Pick 'n Pay stores, over 80 per cent of staff have been allocated shares.

One of Pick 'n Pay's most innovative schemes is our banking scheme, administered by Nedbank under the Pick 'n Pay 'Go Banking' brand. It gives all staff access to safe and reliable banking with lower bank charges, and has enabled many staff members to open and manage savings accounts for the first time. More than R500 million is invested in the banking scheme every year.

The HIV/AIDS pandemic

The charter Pick 'n Pay developed in order to deal with the scourge of HIV/AIDS was designed by our social responsibility team to help our people – and their dependants – as generously, sensibly and humanely as we possibly can. Large amounts of money from external social responsibility funds are also directed at HIV/AIDS education and alleviation programmes throughout South Africa and in neighbouring countries and, at the time of writing, we are mustering resources towards building, equipping and running homes for some of the millions of children who are, and will be, orphaned by the pandemic.

South Africa's people seem to be faced with one epic challenge after another. Of course, we did not expect to replace our troubled past with overnight perfection, but the nature and extent of the HIV/AIDS disaster that plagues South Africa is a cruel blow to a nation that has been through so much.

I have never lost hope in the future of South Africa. Napoleon Bonaparte famously said that 'leaders deal in hope'. My wish has always been to communicate to everyone around me the hope that is intrinsic to my own life. I especially wish to communicate this to the people who are the backbone of our company and to those entrepreneurs starting out on their careers.

Like other epic challenges South Africans have taken on and, indeed, won, I believe that ultimately the HIV/AIDS pandemic will also be conquered. On that, we must pin our unending hope.

Structuring and succession

In the aftermath of the 1994 strike, it became clear that things had gone fundamentally wrong with the way Pick 'n Pay was working. By that time, I had run Pick 'n Pay for 30 years, largely according to my own judgement, intuition and natural inclinations and these had, overall, worked out very well. But the strike of 1994 had caused a sea change in the company: not only had we suffered our first ever drop in sales but morale had taken a dreadful knock and the unruly behaviour of striking workers had damaged the reputation we had so painstakingly built.

When I began to analyse the situation, looking for a way forward, I realised that trouble had, in fact, been building insidiously for quite some time. Financially, growth had been unremarkable since 1991, margins had fallen, as had profitability, measured by return on assets.

Clearly, what was needed was a 'fresh' pair of eyes to take an objective look at Pick 'n Pay as the company stood in 1994. We needed advice from professional consultants who could look through the layers unencumbered by the constraints of history and personal relationship that coloured my own observations.

Bain & Company, an Australian consultancy, were chosen to take on the task of restructuring, and the choice proved to be an excellent one. With their professional eyes and ears, they pointed out that the management structure I had in place had not worked well and recommended splitting the company into two divisions, each with its own main board and management team. The objective was to accelerate moves into the mass market while continuing to nurture and grow the company's traditional middle-class market.

One division, called Pick 'n Pay Retailers, was to be headed by Sean Summers. This division was to oversee the engine room of Pick 'n Pay – our core supermarket and hypermarket chain. The other, Pick 'n Pay Group Enterprises, was placed under my elder son, Gareth, to focus on the enterprise side of the business. Under his control fell the Score Supermarket chain we had acquired the previous year, franchising operations, homeware chain Boardmans, cash-and-carry chain Price Club, new developments outside Africa and new business within.

René de Wet moved into the position of Deputy Chairman at this stage, a role to which he brought his familiar blend of calm good judgement, loyally supporting me until his retirement in 1999.

Although these changes represented the greatest departure from accepted practice within the company since its inception, I thought the plan brilliant, dealing as it did with two sets of problems that had hampered the company's progress persistently – one relating to market position and the other to structure.

When details of the 1994 restructuring were released, I told the press that although I had no immediate intention of hanging up my boots, I was happy to be making way for a younger generation. I knew that Sean and Gareth would need guidance, but I would not interfere with the teams they were to lead, nor would I proffer advice unless it was asked for.

After a somewhat uneasy period, during which I often found myself caught between Sean and Gareth as they tested their new roles, I believed that the restructuring of 1994 was working well both for the company and its leadership and that we were now free to concentrate on both the vexing problems and the exhilaration of trading in the newly democratic South Africa. It was a vote for youth, and as such it succeeded.

Succession planning

In 1999, my son Gareth decided, for personal reasons, that he no longer wished to be part of the executive running of Pick 'n Pay, a decision that plunged us again into a turmoil of leadership concerns.

As a result, after a short period of much confusion and disarray, we announced the appointment of non-family member Sean Summers as CEO of Pick 'n Pay. I remained Executive Chairman and Gareth became my deputy in a non-executive capacity. The new structure of Pick 'n Pay was well received by financial analysts, who applauded a difficult decision taken in the best interests of the company. Appointing Sean Summers to the CEO position put control of the everyday running of the company – at a time when we were doing so much better than analysts believed was possible in the trying economic conditions prevailing – in the hands best qualified for the job.

My point in raising this issue here, in a book that is essentially an attempt to share my personal business philosophy, is to illustrate that with leadership comes tribulation. What you hope for is the wisdom and the fortitude to put aside close personal loyalties to do what is best, not only for shareholders, but for all the people whose livelihoods depend upon your decisions.

When I first consulted with Genus Resources Inc., around 1996, the issue of family succession was a rare discipline and Genus, one of the world's first such consultancies, was in the vanguard of what was destined to become a thriving industry in itself. Today, there are approximately 15 specialist family succession consultancies in the USA alone. The industry came into its own as a result of burgeoning incidences of crisis in family enterprises during the late 1970s and '80s, but latterly succession planning has become an integral part of corporate governance. Companies and their shareholdings are judged, assessed and valued according to the quality of the succession plans in place.

Family succession in high-profile businesses was, for a long time, labelled according to the European idiom that 'the first generation creates, the second inherits and the third destroys' – a sentiment I must immediately dispute, especially being a third-generation businessman myself. Although I did not inherit business interests, I gained the infinitely more valuable attributes of instinct and knowledge from my father and grandfather.

Richard L. Narva, a Genus family succession authority, once stated: 'The heritage of a family connects the experience of its past to the promise of its future.'

Narva termed family businesses 'the greatest secret never told, or at best never reported', but there can be no doubt that the special problems that apply in the case of families planning for a second and third generation who will one day inherit from a founder necessitate diligent and detailed planning in the extreme. There is no single magic moment when leadership and power effortlessly shift from one generation to another.

Founders of family firms, being the creators, the manufacturing, merchandising or operating brain behind the success of the business, exert a singular kind of authority over succession proceedings. Founders also unconsciously become the benchmark against which family members who work in the business are measured: if the second generation fails, they are 'not like [as good as] the first'; if they succeed, it is because of nepotism. I well remember how it felt to be in such a no-win situation; my performance was once assessed against my being Gus Ackerman's son, working my way up through the ranks of Greatermans after they bought my father's Ackermans chain.

Experience and my deep attachment to my family have made me particularly sensitive to the progress of my own children in their careers with Pick 'n Pay. I think I have put more work into succession planning than any other South African family business founder.

The negatives that can attach to family-run businesses – the personality clashes, the possibilities for jealousy, in-fighting and so on – must be read against the positives, of which there are so many. Families might fight, but they also have an enormous capacity for supporting one another. Companies controlled by families that rely on their core values and their relationship skills can be, and often are, formidably successful.

The perception of family-run businesses as archaic units, hidebound and hamstrung by relationships that sit ill with contemporary business aspiration and achievement, is no longer necessarily correct. All over the world, strong family-run businesses have staged a return to optimum performance after the hiccoughs and uncertainties of the 1970s and '80s.

Good intentions and a desire to run a business according to the core values and ethics to which a family subscribes, require formal statements of intent if those good intentions are to be validated and made workable.

As I have mentioned, I have worked incredibly hard with my family, under the direction of the Genus consultancy, to craft the source documents for our family's business legacy. The following excerpt forms the Preamble to the Ackerman Family Constitution – the fruit of all our efforts:

> 'We, the Ackerman family, resolve to work together to ensure the continued profitability and vitality of the Ackerman Family Interests.
>
> 'We, the members of the Ackerman family, while recognising each other's individuality and respecting any differences of opinion which may arise, do personally commit ourselves to work together in the interests in such a manner that will promote total harmony.
>
> 'We, the Ackerman family, recognise that harmony is essential for the continuation and growth of the Ackerman Family Interests.'

In all the efforts I have put into succession plans for Pick 'n Pay, it has never been my intention to rule from the grave but to ensure that the company I will one day hand on will have the strength – through the cohesive and equitable family constitution that is in place, and through having the best, professional, non-family management – to retain its premier position and continue to trade according to the core values and ethics on which it has been built and sustained for so long.

In so far as having the best, professional management is concerned, the appointment in 1999 of non-family member Sean Summers as the CEO was recognised by financial analysts as being in the very best interests of all stakeholders. Sean has done wonderful things for the company and will certainly continue to do so.

The succession planning my family and I have put in place for those members of the family who work within Pick 'n Pay takes care of a 20- to 25-year period after my retirement from active management. It is agreed that, on my death or retirement, my son-in-law David Robins will take on the mantle of chairmanship for five years. At the end of that period, either my daughter Suzanne or my son Jonathan, if ready, will assume the Chair, depending on who is considered most ready by the family and the Board. The family member who does not succeed at that time undertakes to work assiduously towards acceding to the chairmanship five years later.

It has been shown conclusively that family-controlled enterprises that endure, do so when the family is focused on the continuity of its legacy and its core values. When issues around succession are satisfactorily resolved in such a way as to serve the best interests of all, then the family focus can fall on maintaining a set of leadership roles that are grounded in the heritage and values of the family.

An important part of the process of Succession Planning involves recognising that, however earnest and dedicated individual family members might be, both their abilities and their inclinations must be sensitively assessed before an acceptable succession format can be achieved. In exactly the same way as every employee is not cut out to fulfil the same role within an organisation, so every member of a family is, first and foremost, an individual. While some family members may possess the qualities and talents normally required of an active, big-organisation CEO, others may not be comfortable with the pressures of such a role.

In the organisational structures that now exist for our family and for Pick 'n Pay, I see daily evidence of how well and how harmoniously individuals have grown into their roles. Richard Narva also commented that 'between the family and the business, the larger reality is the family'. Certainly, particularly since the events of 1999, during which my elder son Gareth decided to take on a non-executive role within Pick 'n Pay, my family has learned to face realities and reshape our expectations to accommodate individual perceptions of destiny; we have learned to celebrate diversity as a strength.

In the present-day structuring of the company, Gareth remains an active member on all the Boards. As Chairman of Pikwik, he carries huge responsibility in controlling the family holding in Pick 'n Pay, for which the family is extremely grateful. Having Gareth to look after the family affairs with his own competency and flair takes a great deal of weight off my shoulders.

Given the excellence, the drive and the proven ability to defy predictions of doom, those uniquely South African qualities abundantly present in the people who are the backbone of the Fourth Leg of our Table and in the people we serve, I am confident that the legacy I shall leave will allow Pick 'n Pay – the company that has built a business model out of the philosophy of placing giving above getting – not only to survive, but to thrive way into the future all South Africans share.

Fourth Leg points to remember

- The Fourth Leg of the Table contains the 'corporate soul' of a company.
- Making people feel important as individuals is an excellent way to build a business.

- At an employment interview, only the good is on view and the warts remain firmly under wraps – a sound reason for promoting from within.
- The flatter a company's organisational chart, the better the company will be.
- Pick 'n Pay has grown as a company through growing people.
- Astute cash management under the First Leg of the Table funds excellent staff benefits, share schemes, bursaries, housing loans, training and education under the Fourth Leg.
- In the vital area of succession planning 'the heritage of a family connects the experience of its past to the promise of its future'.

Problem-solving

Having traced (in Part I) the origins of the ideas and
philosophies built into our model of the Four Legs of the
Table, and having shown (in Part II) how those principles
were applied to building and sustaining Pick 'n Pay, creating
in the process particular points of difference, it is time to
share details of a very simple, very sane, three-route
problem-solving system that may be successfully applied to
any endeavour.

By diligently following the three-route system
described here:

■ Route 1: Identifying the problem
■ Route 2: Setting objectives
■ Route 3: Formulating a plan of action

and answering the seven questions – What? Where? Why?
When? Which? How? and Who? – contained in the third
route of the plan, you are likely to identify possible pitfalls
and lay a sound foundation for further planning. Cobwebs
and confusion can be replaced by clarity and a new clutch

of the kind of plucky, innovative entrepreneurs for which South Africa is famous can emerge, knowing where it is that they want to go – and the path to follow to get there.

This is the formula I once used to help me decide what I should do when I had reached a particular crossroads in my life. It is how I decided to start my own chain of supermarkets, a decision that came to fruition when, in 1967, I purchased the four small Cape Town-based stores already called Pick 'n Pay.

As Viktor Frankl pointed out, struggling to do something while nagged by the thought that you should be doing something different, dooms all effort to futility. My father, Gus Ackerman, once made precisely the same point, more prosaically: Why waste time climbing mountains when what you really want is to play golf.

10

A way forward

ONE MORNING IN 1966, when I was 35 years old, I woke to find that overnight I had taken up residence in an alien land – the uncharted territory of the unemployed.

The previous morning, I had woken up as General Manager of the Checkers chain of super-markets, and gone off to work as the confident, enthusiastic young man I was. I had good reason to be confident and enthusiastic, too, for I had played a part in building Checkers supermarkets from an uncertain base of four small stores into a thriving chain of 85 outlets for the Greatermans Group, then owners of Checkers.

Checkers, on the day before my life turned upside down, had become South Africa's premier supermarket chain. The board of Greatermans had shown courage and foresight in committing funds to the building of a food chain during the 1950s and '60s – a turbulent time in the history of South Africa when the future was masked in uncertainty. Nevertheless, the challenge was taken and, with Greatermans providing the cash backing, I flew around, as General Manager, working with commitment and conviction, opening Checkers supermarkets across the length and breadth of South Africa.

> It is because I know just how it feels to lose your job, to feel rudderless and helpless, that I empathise with the many similarly placed people who have come to see me over the intervening years, desperate to find a way forward.

In keeping with Bernardo Trujillo's dictum – *When your ear's so close to the ground the grasshoppers can jump in, then you know you're really listening* – I had put my ear to the ground and listened and listened at seminars in the USA, bringing back to South Africa the knowledge with which to build the Checkers chain for Greatermans. Being a loyal and committed 'company man' in every sense of the phrase, I believed I was doing my life's work as a Greatermans employee.

As it turned out, however, success secured neither my career nor my future, as I was to discover when I was suddenly and inexplicably fired in 1966 – a bitter, humiliating and frightening experience that I have never forgotten. It is because I know just how it feels to lose your job, to feel rudderless and helpless, that I empathise with the many similarly placed people who have come to see me over the intervening years, desperate to find a way forward.

It was out of adversity that I had to pick up the pieces and put them together again in the shape of an income-earning occupation – and urgently at that, as I was not well off financially. My recently deceased father had left me a small inheritance, but in the main I had lived since leaving university on a monthly salary which, with a growing family to support, had never accumulated.

In response to the situation in which I found myself after being ousted from Greatermans, I sat down to draw up a plan that would identify the problem and explore options in order to find some solution to my pressing dilemma. I tried to identify all the possible causes of the problem.

Out of this exercise a formula evolved – a formula that pointed me in the direction of starting my own chain of stores. It is a formula that I still use constantly, one I have shared with countless others who have come to ask my counsel in times of confusion.

The three-route formula

Whenever I work through the three-route problem-solving formula, I am vividly reminded of a young Russian woman who once came to see me in a state of despair similar to mine in 1966.

The young woman's troubles had started after her Russian husband decided that the better life he sought to build in South Africa would be better still without his wife and their child: accordingly, he had abandoned them. Penniless, unemployed and without any means of support, she was grimly determined not to return to Russia but rather to find some means of earning a living sufficient to provide for herself and her child. Her first attempt at achieving this goal had not succeeded, adding to her feeling of desperation and failure. Consequently, by the time she came to see me, as a last resort, she harboured a deep suspicion and distrust of her fellow human beings – although she retained her resolve not to return to Russia.

We sat down together with three sheets of blank paper, and started to identify the precise problem. This exercise showed that the *primary* problem was not that her husband had abandoned her (this was the cause of her problem). The answer to the question, 'What is the problem?' was, rather, that she needed to find a way to generate an income that required no capital outlay but that would provide a home and a living for her and her child in South Africa.

Once the real problem was identified, the next stage was to set an objective towards which to work.

Having established that her most marketable attribute was her faultless command of four Slavic languages in addition to excellent English and her native Russian, the tourism industry immediately leaped off the page. Tourists from Russia and Eastern Europe emerged seamlessly as the obvious group from whom income might be earned but, lacking the resources to study towards a tourism qualification, how was she to profit from her talent as a linguist?

By asking seven key questions – what, where, why, when, which, how and who (the Seven Friends Tried and True, with apologies to Rudyard Kipling for the adaptation) – we decided that she should market herself to travel organisations throughout the country as a consultant specialising in liaison between Eastern European and Russian travel organisations and their South African counterparts in order to develop two-way tourism between those countries. All that would initially be required was rented accommodation and a telephone – and these she already had.

One contact, I felt certain, would inevitably lead to another and surely the exigencies of her life – the need to support herself and her child – would translate into the drive necessary to launch and sustain the new enterprise.

Applying the formula

The Russian woman left my offices that day bearing triumphantly the three sheets of paper on which we had found a way forward for her, glowing with hope and enthusiasm, both of which, it turned out, were well founded.

A little over a year later, she came back, glowing again – only this time flushed with success. Caught up in the endless pressures of running Pick 'n Pay and having anyway seen numerous other people who sought solutions, I had wondered only fleetingly in the interim how my once-distraught linguistic visitor had fared.

The answer was that she had fared extraordinarily well. As a token of thanks, she put a small lacquered tray on my conference desk – where it remains to this day – and proceeded to tell me how, from humble beginnings at home with her telephone, she had gone on to establish her own highly successful consultancy, which employed staff and was established in up-market premises. She told me how, during the whirlwind year that had passed since our first meeting, she had bought a lovely house and car, and funded a private education for her child, while comfortably financing her business. Within just one year, her reputation was so well established that when travel people in South Africa and abroad thought of Eastern Europe and Russia, they automatically thought of her.

It was a wonderful story, but what interested me most was that this erstwhile penniless and abandoned person, once devoid of hope, told me that she had not only kept the three sheets of paper on which we once worked out a way forward for her, but had had them framed to hang on her office wall.

Applying the formula to Pick 'n Pay

The problem-solving formula set down here paved the way towards my acquisition of Pick 'n Pay, and I have continued to apply it ever since, particularly when I need to troubleshoot one of the many new directions in which we at Pick 'n Pay have moved over the years.

For example, when the company's Group Enterprises division was in the process of launching the Franchise Division, there was considerable difference of opinion among planners on how to supply future franchisees. For the most part, those involved in deciding the details of the scheme believed that it would be best to supply future franchisees from stocks held in central warehouses, whereas I thought deliveries should be made to the back doors of franchise stores, just as they were made generally to the existing network of stores.

The matter was argued back and forth for quite some time, opposing sides each holding that their preferred system of delivery would smooth the journey towards break-even in the fledgling new division. Being a team player at heart, it was unusual for me to persist as vehemently as I did that I was right, but insist I did. Relegating the issue to and answering questions in the third-route 'how' component of the problem-solving formula had clearly demonstrated that mine was the best course.

As a result, there is absolutely no doubt that Pick 'n Pay avoided making the costly mistake of taking on all the problems and liabilities inherent in operating large and expensive central warehousing facilities on our own. All operational aspects of our Franchise Division were subjected to the scrutiny of the 'Seven Friends Tried and True', which contributed to an earlier than expected breakeven position for the division.

More recently, directors charged with promoting Pick 'n Pay's Australian acquisition settled down to debate the way forward. Conceding that the 75-strong Australian chain was on budget and running well, we nevertheless pondered the best way forward for the chain into the future.

In discussions, a strong body of opinion held that buying through a secondary supplier for the Australian stores was hindering expansion. Suddenly, as debate went back and forth on the merits of breaking away from the secondary supplier and opening our own independent warehouses in Australia, I realised that we had lost sight of the primary cause of our problem. What we actually needed to do was to define afresh the best ways in which to take our Australian venture forward, only one part of which concerned the issue of warehousing. The issue of the secondary supplier as opposed to owned warehouses was a cause, but not the primary problem – which was that we were failing to see an all-encompassing, clear way forward.

Only once we got back to asking basic questions – for example, Do we have enough stores? Do we have enough growth? – was the plan for our future trading in Australia redefined and subsequently implemented.

Applying the formula to succession planning

One very important area in which the formula should be meticulously applied is that of succession planning, a pivotal issue in family-owned businesses. I had already begun to think deeply around this question as early as 1985 when, in the vanguard of contemporary business thinking, I decided to consult with Genus Resources, then one of just a few such professional consultants.

The crisis in standards of corporate morals visible in the last decade of the twentieth century nudged governments around the world towards making succession planning an integral part of corporate governance. Therefore, in family-run businesses today, having a quality succession plan in place determines criteria against which the company is judged, assessed and valued. My belief in the virtues of sound succession planning long pre-dates, however, the relevant legislation. I have no wish to 'rule from the grave', but I did want the core values and ethics on which the company was built and is sustained to be identified and codified in a document to which the entire Ackerman family subscribes.

Using the first route of the formula, I was able to identify the nature of the 'problem' – in this case less of a problem than a challenge: What was causing the 'problem' and what might the solutions be? Going down the second route, I identified my objectives in wishing to formulate and adopt a family constitution. Finally, I conversed with the Seven Friends Tried and True in the third route in order to formulate a precise plan of action for reaching that objective.

As each of the preceding examples shows, the problem-solving formulae in the following chapter – a practical guide – can be applied as easily to an actual problem as to a broad area of decision, or to form a first-stage business plan as I did when starting my own chain.

The three-route plan, particularly when applied to practicalities around starting a new business, clears away confusion and helps formulate an informed decision. Through applying the formulae diligently it should also be possible to cut through the clutter, so to speak, that may have been impeding progress.

11

A practical guide

On a large sheet of blank paper write down the following:

Route 1: Identifying the nature of the problem

Step 1: What is the problem?

Identifying the problem and keeping it separate from its causes takes honesty and self-discipline. Listing causes rather than the problem itself is an easy mistake to make, perhaps because the immediacy of the causes makes them most prominent. The man who tells me his problem is that his wife is always angry with him, that no one respects him, is not identifying a problem but rather its causes. The problem in this instance is lack of money, which causes resentment, debt and a lack of respect.

Using a process of honest evaluation, eliminate subsidiaries until you reach a single primary problem. Examples of primary problems are:

➤ I have no money.
➤ I need a job.
➤ I have married the wrong man/woman.
➤ I want to start a business of my own.
➤ I have no direction.
➤ I hate my job.

Summary of Problem-solving guide

Route 1

Write down on your first blank sheet of paper:
1. What is the problem?
2. What are the causes of the problem?
3. What are possible solutions to the problem?

Route 2

Write down on your second blank sheet of paper:
1. What is/are my objective/s?
2. How do I reach my objective/s?

Route 3

List on a third blank sheet of paper every question you can think of under the headings:

What? Where? Why? When? Which? How? Who?

Answer every question you can possibly think of under Route 3 and you should end up with all the major components necessary for drawing up a plan of action.

Step 2: What are the causes of the problem?

Having clearly identified the precise nature of the problem, write down a list of causes (X) of the problem (Y) and the results (Z). At this stage, remember again the fundamental difference between the problem (Y) and the causes of the problem (X). A list of causes might include some of the following:

➤ I am inadequately qualified (X).

➤ I wanted to be self-employed (Y) and am, therefore, miserable (Z).

➤ I constantly disagree with management actions (Y) because I believe there is a better way (X).

> ➤ I have never felt truly committed to my career (X).
> ➤ I am increasingly in debt (Z) because I am unemployed (Y).
> ➤ My family belittles me (Z) because I have a subservient job that I hate (Y). (Your family does not belittle you because you have a subservient job, but rather because having a subservient job has eroded your confidence and taught you to expect the same of others as you expect of yourself. The reactions and attitudes of others result from the primary problem.)
> ➤ I am constantly worried (Z) because I have lost my job (Y). (The primary problem here is not that you are constantly worried because you have lost your job, but rather that you are constantly worried by what has happened since you became unemployed.)
> ➤ I am pervaded by a feeling of pointlessness (Z) because my husband bullies me (Y).
> ➤ I have been retrenched (Y) because the company has been restructured (X).
> ➤ I have been dismissed (Y) because having to catch two buses makes me late for work (X).
> ➤ I married too young (Y) because I was without direction (X).

Step 3: What are possible solutions to the problem?

With both the primary problem and its consequences identified, list possible solutions, of which there will probably be at least seven or eight. List possible solutions in order of preference, allocating each a mark out of 10.

Finally, choose one.

Possible solutions are:
> ➤ Investigate leaders in my chosen field and research how I might join them.
> ➤ Start my own small business. (In my own case the one point that shone through with persistent clarity was that I knew absolutely that I wished to pursue the ideals of consumer sovereignty suggested by my mentors.)
> ➤ Go back to university.
> ➤ Pick a field of expertise in which I can work on my own (What are my talents? What am I especially good at?).
> ➤ Emigrate.

➤ Found a business based on dealing with my own adversity. In other words make a virtue of adversity. What can be learned from your circumstances?

➤ Establish independence through controlling my own income.

➤ Study by correspondence, and fund this through part-time work.

➤ Find ways to fund doing what I know in my heart will satisfy and fulfil me. What do I love doing?

In the case of the exercise I set myself after losing my job in 1966, I listed as potential solutions to my primary problem (which was being unemployed):

➤ … to go back to university to retrain for a new profession

➤ … to find a new job with a company that would welcome my expertise

➤ … to emigrate

➤ … to stay with food retailing, but start my own small supermarket chain, with the ideal of pursuing my over-riding and ever-present objective of promoting consumer sovereignty.

Now take a second blank sheet of paper and put down:

Route 2 : Setting objectives

Step 1: What is/are my objective(s)?

Your goal may have always been in the forefront of your mind and there may thus be no hesitation in defining your objective(s). It may be, however, that through following the three steps of Route 1 an objective will become clear that might otherwise not have been apparent.

Examples of objectives are:

➤ I aim to find an occupation that will take my family out of poverty and give them something worthwhile.

➤ My objective is to have a happy and fulfilled life and, therefore, making money might be a reward rather than a goal.

➤ I aim to be financially independent.

➤ I aim to be a world authority on cheetah conservation.

When it came to selecting a final objective in my own case, the work I had done in Route 1 had already made it perfectly plain that I wanted to stay in retailing and in food retailing in particular. My progression from Professor Hutt's teachings on the primacy of consumer sovereignty to Bernardo Trujillo's explanation of how that idea translated into business sense – business with a conscience – had become the creed by which I worked, and the goal to which I aspired.

The objective I therefore chose – because the process that had gone before pointed me clearly in this direction – was 'to find a financially rewarding career that would also allow me to promote the ideals of consumer sovereignty'.

Step 2: How do I reach my objective/s?

This is the stage where the solutions to the primary problem begin to match up with the chosen objective. For example: I want to lead a happy and fulfilled life, but how do I reach that objective?

Should I
- ➤ … open my own small business?
- ➤ … go and live in the Namibian desert where cheetahs abound?
- ➤ … convert to Islam?
- ➤ … leave my husband?
- ➤ … return to university?

By clearing the mind in order to get to the basic problem, looking at causes and solutions, identifying an objective (goal or mission) and deciding how to achieve it (to which there will a series of answers), a clear answer to the fundamental question, 'What is it that I really want to do?', should leap off the two pages worked through as Routes 1 and 2.

The next process provides the means of practical implementation in a beautifully simple – but entirely effective – format.

On a third sheet of paper, write down the following:

Route 3: Formulating a plan of action

While Routes 1 and 2 should have made clear what it is you 'really want to do', you now need to formulate a plan of action, with the help of our Seven Friends Tried and True:

What?

For example:

➤ What should I do?

➤ What type of enterprise or activity shall I start?

➤ What is it that really makes me happy?

Where?

For example:

➤ Where shall I work?

➤ Where is the best place to locate my enterprise?

➤ Where is there an under-concentration of the service I plan to offer?

➤ Where am I happiest living?

➤ Where are my family's needs best met?

Why?

In answering, 'Why am I doing this?', you need to return to the objective and say to yourself:

'I'm doing this because

➤ I need to make money

➤ there is a definite gap in the market

➤ I could do this better and more efficiently than those already doing it.'

When?

In deciding when you should start your enterprise, you need to consider, for example:

- ➤ Should I first go back to university and study?
- ➤ Should I start immediately?
- ➤ Should I wait for a specific event in order to promote my launch more effectively?

Which?

Consider which format best fits your plans. For example:

- ➤ Should I join up with somebody and form a partnership?
- ➤ Should I try to buy an existing business?
- ➤ Should I start from scratch?

How?

For example:

- ➤ How will I finance my plan?
- ➤ How am I going to live until I start to make money?
- ➤ How will I promote my service?
- ➤ How shall I go about researching existing services for purposes of comparison?
- ➤ How will my proposed enterprise operate logistically?

Who?

For example:

- ➤ Who will be my customers?
- ➤ Who will be my first colleagues?
- ➤ Who will be my accountant, my bankers, my lawyers?

12

Success in business

WITH THE SHRINKING of formal avenues of employment in South Africa only a slim minority of school leavers now find employment in the formal sector of the South African economy – young people starting out, or people who have been retrenched, have little choice but to become self-employed entrepreneurs in order to earn a living.

> At times, indeed, the more barren the ground in which the seed of a new enterprise is planted, the more abundant the crop.

While the challenges facing new enterprise in South Africa today are different from the challenges I faced when I started trading for my own account in 1967, no period in time is totally devoid of risk. At times, indeed, the more barren the ground in which the seed of a new enterprise is planted, the more abundant the crop.

For example, the supermarket industry started in the USA when war and one of the most severe economic depressions in the history of the modern world created a crying need for cash-strapped people to access cheap food. The mass food marketing pioneers of the USA created an advantage out of disadvantage and, in so doing, revolutionised the distribution, marketing and pricing of food and launched a giant, global industry.

Each generation of entrepreneurs believes that things were easier for those who went before. My father's generation, among whom were the first mass retail traders of early twentieth-century southern Africa, might have started out at a time of pioneering expansion and abundant opportunity, but they came – almost without exception – from penniless immigrant refugee families; they also had little or no education and were obliged to trade. And this they did – with great flair and dash, through the Great Depression, two world wars and major political and social ructions on the African continent.

In 1967, it is true to say that the South African economy was thriving, having experienced an economic boom of unprecedented proportions. But there was another, less auspicious, side to the coin: in the midst of the economic upswing of the 1960s, the South African political climate in which I found myself angling to acquire Pick 'n Pay was always threatening to fragment, go adrift, unravel into chaos.

Towards the end of 1966, when I went knocking on the bank manager's door in search of finance to buy Pick 'n Pay, the peculiar circumstances governing the day-to-day life and the politics of South Africa had made the '60s a difficult decade through which to live and to trade.

Then again, I went looking for funds as an unemployed man, a man, furthermore, whose dismissal had caused considerable speculation in financial circles. People wondered why a company would fire a man who had crafted a huge retail success for them – unless there was more to the dismissal than met the eye ...? My acquisition of Pick 'n Pay was ultimately funded partly with a conventional loan and partly unconventionally – with an issue of shares to raise shareholder capital.

Whatever the formula I chose to put into action, however, I still recall the tension of the few fraught days during which I had to raise the money to purchase Pick 'n Pay. However, what I still know is that I would have done whatever it took to raise that money.

Donny Gordon, globally famed for his remarkable, entrepreneurial business brain, once admitted that the hardest thing he ever had to do was to persuade friends and contacts to invest stakes in the capital of R10 000 he needed to found what became the Liberty business empire – a giant of South African business, eventually valued at billions of rands.

Almost without exception, people who wish to start a business, especially young people, lament the difficulty of raising capital. While I certainly do not seek to minimise the magnitude of such difficulties, I firmly believe that prospective entrepreneurs will do well to remember the words of Bernardo Trujillo: *Starting a business takes 10 per cent capital and 90 per cent guts.*

As, indeed, it truly does.

However insurmountable the problem of funding appears to be, remember that this is merely 10 per cent of what is required in order to start an enterprise. Given a single-minded conviction of the viability of an idea and a passion for pursuing a certain path; given dedication, perseverance, integrity and a goal that goes beyond the mere making of money, no force – certainly not the 10 per cent factor of finding the money – will ever prove powerful enough to thwart a dream.

If seekers of start-up funding today find that their innovative ideas and business plans fail to impress formal lending institutions, I would advise them to look for less usual, more creative, ways of financing the new venture rather than losing heart and abandoning what might be a great idea. Take heart from the early fund-raising challenges of numerous hugely successful businesspeople and ask 10 family members or friends, for instance, to each lend R1 000 towards start-up capital. There are many funding avenues that can be explored. As long as seekers of capital remain persistent in resolve and passionate about the goal, some form of funding opportunity *will* present itself.

In summary, then, there follows a list of 10 action steps, some applying to retail but others applicable to the successful running of any type of enterprise. They have stood me in good stead.

10 STEPS TO SUCCESS

- **Start out with a clear business plan**. The three-route formula I have described here is one I use all the time to solve the problem at hand.
- **Focus on a pinhead**. Don't try to do too many things at once. Concentrate on one venture.
- **Listen to advice and ideas** – even from the humblest individual. Too many people are too conscious of their own importance to listen to the advice of others. Your ear should be so close to the ground that grasshoppers can jump in!
- **Have a Mission Statement** designed to identify the object of your endeavour. This is not merely the stuff of which slogans are made; it translates into a tangible business mission and objective.
- **Don't give up on a great idea** because you don't have the money to start. It takes 90 per cent guts and only 10 per cent capital.
- **Cash liquidity is absolutely critical** when running any business. If you have to borrow, ensure that your business has a good cash flow before you do so; many businesses fail not because people lack ideas, energy or commitment but simply because there is insufficient actual cash to operate satisfactorily on a day-to-day basis.
- **Social responsibility** should run through the veins of any good business person as a positive life force. Having a well-defined commitment to social responsibility is a form of enlightened self-interest but at the end of the day, it does not matter what actually motivates social responsibility policies. What does matter is that good deeds and funding go to causes that really need them – and that is the real, the only, justification necessary.
- **Answer every call and reply to every message and letter** on a daily basis. No query or complaint is too small for the top person's attention and every interaction must be handled with courtesy and decisiveness.
- **Do not price everything in the same margin**. Too many businesses put the same gross margin on every line, and then wonder why they fail to attract customers.
- **It never pays to argue with a customer**. Take back goods graciously and without question. Even if you harbour the suspicion that the customer is at fault, or if the goods the customer wants to return may have been purchased elsewhere, be 'big-minded' – and build a great business.

Some 38 years after we started to build it, Pick 'n Pay continues to flourish in terms of results; it continues to maintain the core values, standards and commitment to consumer sovereignty, in the face of formidable expansion and turbulent times, for which our company is so proud to be known. We have, however, weathered our fair share of trials and tribulations, for no time is ever without them.

Young entrepreneurs starting out today face fierce challenges of their own, and have huge hurdles to clear. South Africa's successful transition from the rule of apartheid to democracy in 1994 left the whole world gasping in admiration. That precious democracy holds as strong and proud as ever but, a decade on, it is necessary to acknowledge that there are problems too, and it is these challenges – among them the great boot of crime crushing citizens and their enterprises underfoot, and the prevalence of HIV/AIDS and how business will overcome its chilling impact – that South African entrepreneurs must confront and seek to resolve.

It is a tall order to fill, a tough legacy to inherit, but with our history in mind, I am absolutely confident that it can be done – magnificently. Why, after all, would South Africa's citizens have emerged from the maelstrom of the past – somewhat battered and uncertain no doubt, but hanging on to hope and unity – if not to go forward confidently together to tackle the future?

My wish for all new entrepreneurs, but especially for young South Africans of all races, is that their resolve should be followed by fortune, and that their enterprises should thrive.

Index

Page numbers in italics indicate illustrations.